NIBBLES

A collection of quick and easy Hors d'oeuvres, canapes, and Appetizers

By
Suzie Stephens

Artwork and Illustrations
By
Diane Chrenko

Nibbles is dedicated
to my wonderful Aunt

Carolyn Lovell

First printing	Sept. 81	1,000 copies
Second printing	Feb. 82	1,000 copies
Third printing	Feb. 83	5,000 copies

ISBN: 0-9610246-0-7

Published by C.S. Stephens
Printed in U.S.A. by
S. C. Toof & Co.
Memphis, TN

Definitions

According to Webster's New World Dictionary

Ap'pe-tiz'er, n. a tasty food that stimulates the appetite.

ca-na-pé, n. [FR.], a cracker, etc. spread with spiced meat, cheese, etc., served as an appetizer.

hors d'oeuvre (ôr'dūrv,' -duv,' pl., d'oeuvres), [FR.], any of a variety of appetizers, as canapés, olives, etc.

SPECIAL INGREDIENTS

Some people play golf for pleasure and some people collect stamps. I cook for fun. When I'm unhappy, nothing cheers me up faster than creating something delicious in the kitchen. Nothing pleases me more than cooking for people. The more the merrier!

I have enjoyed collecting all of these recipes. Since I cannot invite everyone over for hors d'oeuvres I can at least share some of these recipes with you so you can.

I must thank Jodie Standrod for helping me with Heath and Lauren. She also gave me some great recipes to include in this book.

Diane Chrenko is my talented friend who kept insisting that we could do this book. Deadline or not, we did it Diane!

Jim gave us both encouragement. At times we needed that more than anything. I must thank my dad for all of his support and also Lori Collins for being my friend.

Enjoy,

Suzie

CONTENTS

BEEF BITES

Beef or Chicken Kabobs

1 large sirloin steak cut into 1 inch squares.
OR:
4 de-boned large chicken breasts cut into 1 inch squares
(pour marinade sauce over squares - refrigerate overnight!)

18 small onions (1 inch in diameter or less)
 3 large bell peppers, sliced into ½ inch pieces
24 medium fresh, firm mushrooms
24 cherry tomatoes

—On a 6" - 8" wooden skewer place beef, onion, bellpepper, mushroom, beef, tomato, mushroom, just so there is at least 3 to 4 pieces of meat on the skewer and 2 pepper strips, 2 tomatoes, 2 onions and 2 mushrooms.

—Charcoal or broil until meat is done - maybe 6 minutes on each side.

—The meat has already been marinated -

   (Try a combination of beef & chicken!)

Beefy Cheese Ball

½ lb. cheddar cheese, finely grated
1 tsp. Worchestershire
¼ cup pitted ripe olives, chopped
½ cup dried beef, coarsely chopped
1 3 oz. pkg. softened cream cheese
5 Tbls. Sherry
Dash of onion, garlic, and celery salt
Another 1 cup dried beef, chopped

— Combine all ingredients except for the 1 cup dried beef.

— Roll into ball and refrigerate overnight.

— Before serving, roll ball in dried beef.

Serve with Crackers

Beefy Rotel Dip or Spread

1 can "Rotel" brand tomatoes
1 lb. Velveeta cheese
½ lb. hamburger meat, browned and drained,
   then crumbled.

—Melt cheese in top of double boiler.

—Add crumbled meat and tomatoes to melted
   cheese.

—Serve warm with tortilla chips.

Crunchy Meaty Munchies

1 lb. lean ground beef
½ lb. lean ground pork
2 eggs slightly beaten
½ tsp. salt
¼ cup fine dry breadcrumbs
1 Tbls. soy sauce
¼ tsp. garlic salt
1 (8½ oz.) can waterchestnuts, drained and chopped
1 jar teriyaki sauce

—Combine beef, pork, eggs, salt, breadcrumbs, soy sauce, garlic salt and chopped chestnuts.

—Shape into 1" balls.

—Arrange on rack of broiler pan

—Bake 15 to 18 minutes in preheated 375° oven.

—Brown meatballs thoroughly.

—Drain on paper towels.

—Spear with toothpicks.

—Dip into teriyaki sauce.

Dried Beef Pinwheels

1 3 oz. package cream cheese, softened
2 Tbls. snipped green onions
1 tsp. garlic powder or seasoning salt
1 to 2 Tbls. mayonnaise
¼ lb. sliced dried beef

— Mix cheese, onions, garlic powder, and mayonnaise together.

— Spread 2 slices of beef with mixture and place one on top of the other.

— Roll up tightly and chill several hours or overnight.

— Cut each roll into 1½ to 2 inch slices.

— Insert a toothpick into edge of each slice.

Jalapeno Pepper Tip

If you don't want to set your guests on fire, rinse peppers thoroughly, cut in half or de-seed by cutting tip off pepper - pull membrane out - rinse and pat dry with paper towel. This makes a less peppier pepper!

Meatballs á la Fruit

2 eggs beaten
1 cup chopped mixed dried fruits
  (apricots, prunes, raisins, apples)
½ cup finely chopped onion
½ cup crumbled fresh bread crumbs
1½ tsp. salt
1 dash tabasco
1½ lbs. ground beef
2 Tbls. vegetable oil
1 cup sweet vermouth

— Combine all ingredients, except oil and vermouth, until evenly mixed.

— Shape into 1 inch balls.

— In a large skillet, sauté 1 layer of meatballs at a time in hot oil until evenly browned.

— Place in a heated chafing dish.

— Warm vermouth, pour over all and serve.

Meat Marinade for Chicken or Beef Kabob Appetizers

⅔ cup soy sauce
¼ cup salad oil
6 cloves garlic
2 tsps. monosodium glutamate
2 tsps. ginger
2 tsps. dry mustard
2 tsps. molasses

—Combine all ingredients in a bowl and let stand.

—Pour on beef or chicken, let set for 24 hours before you put meat on skewers.

Mediterranean Meatballs

1 lb. ground beef
1 cup cooked rice
½ cup minced onion
¼ cup snipped fresh dill
¼ cup snipped fresh parsley
1 egg beaten
1 tsp. salt
1/8 tsp. pepper
½ cup flour
1 egg beaten
Vegetable oil

— Combine beef, rice, onion, dill, parsley, egg, salt, and pepper.

— Shape into balls and dip in flour, then eggs.

— Heat 1 inch of oil in a skillet; fry meatballs until golden.

— Serve warm.

Ready Freddies

1 3- to 4-ounce package sliced smoked beef, snipped.
1 4-oz. package shredded Cheddar cheese
1 can pitted ripe olives, sliced
1 cup mayonnaise
Rye crackers

— Mix beef, cheese, olives, and mayonnaise.

— Spread about 1 tablespoon on each rye cracker.

— Bake in a 375⁰ oven for 6 - 8 minutes or until bubbly.

— Serve warm.

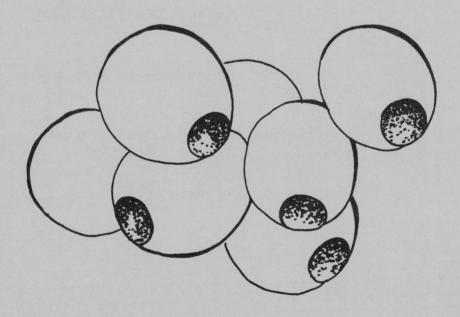

Sauerbraten Meatballs

1 recipe of your favorite All American Swedish Meatballs. (Cut in half)

Sauce:
  1 medium onion grated
  1 tbs. butter
  1¼ cups water
  2 tbs. sugar
  1 cup gingersnaps, crushed
  ½ tbs. salt
  ¼ cup vinegar
  2 bay leaves
  6 whole peppercorns

—Sauté onion in butter until slightly browned.

—Add remaining ingredients and boil until slightly thickened.

—Strain and pour over meatballs in a chafing dish.

Sauce should be thick, but add water if you want to make it thinner.

Use toothpicks to skewer meatballs.

Yum!

Sauerkraut Balls

½ cup onion, chopped
3 Tbls. butter
6 Tbls. flour
1 cup lean ham (ground & cooked)
1 cup ground corned beef
2 cups sauerkraut
1 tsp. dry mustard
1 Tbls. chopped parsley

2 cloves garlic
½ cup sherry
flour
1 egg
½ cup milk
bread crumbs
hot oil

— Sauté onion in butter until soft. Add flour, cook until well blended. Add the 1 cup lean cooked ground ham and the 1 cup corned beef. Add sauerkraut (which has been ground & drained before measuring), dry mustard, parsley, garlic cloves (pressed).

— Add sherry and cook till mixture forms thick paste. Spread on platter to cool and chill well for at least 2 hours.

— Shape mixture into balls the size of a walnut, roll in flour.

— Beat egg, add the milk, dip balls in egg mixture and roll in fine bread crumbs.

— Fry balls in deep hot oil (370⁰) until they are a rich brown.

— Drain on paper towels.

— Serve with frilly toothpicks.

Spicey Beef Stuffed Snow-Peas

½ lb. Chinese pea pods
1 (2½ oz.) pkg. thinly sliced spiced beef
1 tsp. prepared horseradish
1 cup dairy sour cream
½ tsp. prepared mustard
1/8 tsp. pepper

— Trim ends from pea pods.

— Bring 3 cups salted water to a boil in a medium saucepan.

— Carefully lower pea pods into boiling water.

— Simmer over medium heat 1 minute.

— Drain.

— Immediately place pods in cold water.

— Drain and refrigerate until chilled.

— Chop beef until fine.

— In a small bowl combine beef, horseradish, sour cream, mustard, and pepper.

— With a sharp knife carefully slit one side of pea pod.

— Use small spoon and fill each pod with beef mixture.

— Arrange filled pods on baking sheet with raised sides. Refrigerate.

Serve cold.

Stuffed "Meated" Jalapeno Peppers

1 dozen green pickled jalapeno peppers
1 small can potted meat
2 Tbls. chopped sweet pickles
2 Tbls. mayonnaise
½ dozen saltine crackers, crushed

—Mix meat, pickles, mayonnaise and enough cracker crumbs to make a thick paste.

—Cut the tip end off peppers, remove seeds and membrane.

—Stuff peppers with mixture

—Serve as a HOT hors d'oeuvre.

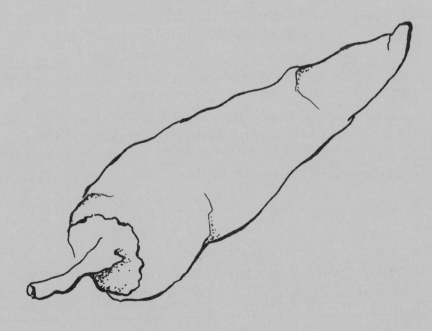

Sweet and Sour Surprises
(this recipe uses not only tiny meatballs but uses shrimp and chicken livers also!)

2 Tbls. cornstarch
2 Tbls. sugar
½ tsp. monosodium glutamate
1 chicken bouillon cube
½ cup water
⅓ cup vinegar
1 cup pineapple juice
2 Tbls. soy sauce
1 Tbls. butter

* * *

½ lb. tiny meatballs cooked
     (if you don't have a favorite
recipe, use ½ recipe for the All
American Swedish Meatballs)
½ lb. shrimp, cooked, peeled & deveined
½ lb. chicken livers, cooked

—Combine first 9 ingredients in sauce pan. Cook and stir until mixture boils & bubbles.

—Cover & simmer 5 minutes

—Group meatballs, shrimp and chicken livers in sauce.

—Heat thoroughly; serve hot in a chafing dish or pretty bowl.

Teriyaki Sirloin Roll ups

⅓ cup soy sauce
2 Tbls. honey
¼ tsp. ground ginger
1 garlic clove, crushed
1 tsp. grated onion
¼ cup dry white wine
¾ lb. boneless top sirloin (partially frozen)
1 (6 oz.) can water chestnuts, drained

—Combine soy sauce, honey, ginger, garlic, onion and wine in a bowl. Set aside.

—Cut meat into thin long slices (like bacon.)

—Cut water chestnuts in half

—Wrap 1 slice meat around each water chestnut half, secure with wooden toothpick.

—Place in a pan so that the roll ups can be marinated with soy mixture. Marinate 1 hour.

—Place roll ups, drained, on a broiler pan.

—Broil meat 3-4 minutes, turning once or twice until they are browned evenly.

—Serve hot!

The All-American Swedish Meatball
(This looks difficult but it isn't; there are a lot of ingredients)

1 lb. sausage
2 lbs. ground chuck
2 tsp. salt
½ tsp. pepper
½ cup catsup

2 tbls. worcestershire
½ cup chopped onion
2 eggs
1 cup corn flakes
1 cup evaporated milk

— Mix all ingredients real well. Shape into balls by using 1 tsp. for each ball. Place into pan and bake for 12-15 minutes at 400. Makes 120 small meat balls.

sauce

2 bottles catsup
1 bottle chili sauce
½ cup prepared mustard
1 tbl. dry mustard
1½ cups white sugar
1 cup wine vinegar
½ cup lemon juice

1 bottle BBQ sauce
Dash of tabasco
½ cup worcestershire
1 tbls. soy sauce
2 tbls. salad oil
1 cup beer
1 clove crushed garlic

— Combine all ingredients and mix well. Heat before storing.

TO SERVE: Heat sauce w/meatballs and place in chafing dish. (makes two batches) Use toothpicks to skewer.

VEGETABLES, ETC.

Artichoke Balls

4 Tbls. olive oil
2 small onions, chopped very fine
1 bulb garlic, chopped very fine
2 cans artichokes
1 eight oz. (large) can parmesan cheese
seasoned "progresso" breadcrumbs

— Sauté onions and garlic on low heat 1 hour

— Let two cans of artichokes drain while onions
and garlic are cooking.

— When onions and garlic are cooling, chop artichokes and mix well with 1 can parmesan
cheese.

— Now add onions & garlic

— Mix all together and roll into small balls then
roll into the bread crumbs.(one inch balls.)

— Refrigerate overnight.

Artichokes in Lemon

1 13 oz. jar artichoke hearts
3 Tbls. lemon juice
2 Tbls. olive oil
1 clove garlic, crushed
1/4 tsp. salt
1/8 tsp. pepper

— Chill artichokes

— Combine remaining ingredients. Pour this
 mixture over artichokes. Let stand till you are
 ready to serve it!

— Serve with toothpicks.

Basic Cocktail Hors D'Oeuvres

36 sword shaped plastic toothpick skewers
1 large can chunk pineapple, drained
36 ½" cubes cheddar cheese
36 stuffed green olives

— On the skewer place one pineapple chunk, then the olive, then the cheese cube.

— Arrange on a tray.

Serve with your favorite drink. So simple & quick.

Tip!

Parsley: Fresh parsley looks great around any plate of hors d'oeuvres. Use it a lot. Be creative!

Cheese Triangles/Tiropetes

1 lb. Filo leaves
1 lb. feta cheese, crumbled (goat cheese)
3 egg yolks
1 cup butter, melted
1 cup grated cheese, (Parmesan)
2 Tbls. chopped parsley
1 cup small curd cottage cheese

—Combine feta cheese, eggs, grated cheese, parsley, 3 Tbls. butter and cottage cheese. Mix well.

—Cut filo sheets into long strips 3 inches wide and brush with melted butter.

—Place 1 tsp. of the cheese mixture at the bottom of each strip and fold the corner up to form a triangle. Continue folding in a triangle shape (like a flag) until entire strip is folded.

—Continue this method until all of the ingredients are used.
—Place triangles on cookie sheets, brush with melted butter.

—Bake them at 375⁰ for 15 to 20 minutes. Serve immediately!

Chutney Canapé Spread

4 hard cooked eggs
1 three oz. pkg. cream cheese
2 Tbls. mayonnaise
1 Tbls. worcestershire
1 Tbls. curry powder
Dash cayenne & tabasco
2 Tbls. chopped chutney

— Mash hard cooked eggs with cream cheese

— Add mayonnaise and seasonings and mix well.

— Add chutney and chill

— Take out of refrigerator in time to soften

— Serve in a hollowed-out bell pepper shell with crackers.

So pretty!

Cocktail Beets

2 one lb. cans small whole beets, drained
1 eight oz. package cream cheese, softened
2 Tbls. horseradish
1 Tbls. mayonnaise

— Combine cream cheese, horseradish, and mayonnaise, mixing well.

— Scoop center out of beets and fill with cream cheese mixture.

— Chill

Cracker Simpletons

Use saltine crackers, "Ritz" crackers or your favorite.

— On one side only brush with melted butter. Sprinkle buttered top with paprika and a touch of parmesan cheese.

— Place in broiler until brown. (Watch carefully -don't burn!)

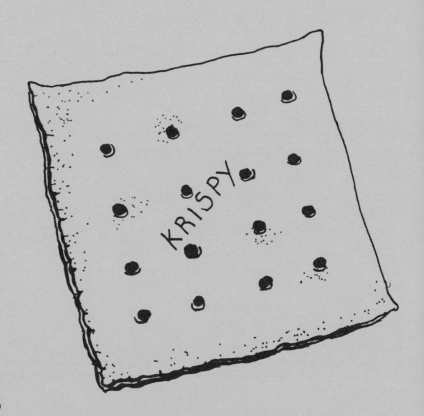

Crispy Potato Skins

— Hollow out baked potatoes so you have the skin left.

— Cut the skins into long strips

— Butter thoroughly

— Sprinkle with salt and pepper and place on cookie sheet in 375^0 - 400^0 oven until crisp.

Try serving them with sour cream & chive dip. They are great by themselves though.

M -m - mm good

Cucumber Cheese Slices

2 medium cucumbers
salt to taste
12 ozs. creamed cheese
2 Tbls. chopped onion
¼ cup chopped green bell pepper
1 Tbls. chopped pimiento
paprika, pepper, and Worcestershire to taste.

—Halve cucumbers lengthwise. Pare. Remove seeds, leaving center hollow. Sprinkle with salt. Let drain.

—Combine cheese, onion, bell pepper, pimiento and paprika in a bowl.

—Season above with salt, pepper & worcestershire.

—Dry cucumber halves, pack firmly with cheese mixture in the hollowed out center. Press halves together (so it looks like a whole cucumber again.) Chill.

—To serve, cut crosswise into ¼ inch slices.

Fish Triangles/Psaropetes

1 cup chopped shrimp and crab
½ cup small curd cottage cheese
1 Tbls. minced parsley
dash of lemon juice
fill pastry sheets
one stick melted butter

— Combine shrimp, crab, cheese, parsley, and lemon juice.

— Cut filo sheets into long strips 3 inches wide and brush with melted butter.

— Follow directions on how to fold filo (according to the Cheese Triangle recipe) placing a teaspoon of the shellfish mixture at the bottom of each strip. (Fold like cheese triangle.)

— Brush with melted butter.

— Bake at 375⁰ for 15 - 20 minutes.

Serve warm.

Tip!

Paprika can jazz up any vegetable or meat hors d'oeuvre. Sprinkle it on plain cucumber slices or on lemon wedges or even on cold pack cheese spreads!

Garlic Ripe Olives

1 nine oz. can ripe olives
olive oil
2 cloves garlic, halved
½ cup cracked ice

— Drain olives. Put in bowl. Cover with olive oil
to depth of ¼". Stir in garlic & ice.

— Cover. Let stand at room temperature 2 to 3
hours.

— Drain before serving.

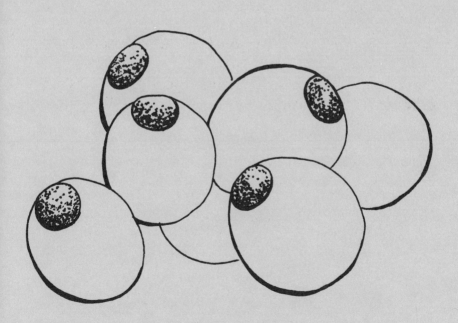

Gourmet Relish Tray

1 jar pickled okra
1 jar marinated artichoke hearts
1 jar pickled baby corn
1 jar pickled mushrooms
1 jar stuffed olives
1 jar black olives
1 pint cherry tomatoes

— Arrange above on a tray covered with lettuce leaves.

— Be creative in the arrangement.

— Think color.

— Think geometric shapes.

(Don't forget to drain all of the above well.)

Decorate with pretty frilly toothpicks. Serve crackers on the side.

Lush Mush

1 box mushrooms
2 - 3 Tbls. butter
2 Tbls. dry sherry
2 Tbls. bourbon whiskey

—Clean mushrooms and remove stems

—Sauté mushrooms in butter in a skillet over low heat

—When heated through, add sherry.

—When cooking is finished, add bourbon.

Serve warm - use toothpicks to spear the Lush -Mush.

Meat Triangles/Kreatopetes

1 cup chopped or ground meat
2 Tbls. grated cheese (Parmesan)
1 hard boiled egg, finely chopped
Filo pastry sheets
1 stick melted butter

— Sauté meat.

— Add cheese and egg to meat.

— Place a teaspoon of the mixture at the bottom of the filo strips (follow directions as for Cheese Triangles).

— Brush with melted butter.

— Bake at 375° for 15 to 20 minutes.

Serve warm.

Mushroom Capers

18 - 24 large mushrooms, washed and dried
1/3 cup fine dry bread crumbs
1 Tbls. lemon juice
1/8 tsp. garlic powder
1/8 tsp. rosemary
1/8 tsp. marjoram
1/4 tsp. salt
1/4 cup almonds, finely chopped
1 Tbls. capers, minced
butter
parsley

— Chop mushroom stems and combine with remaining ingredients

— Spoon mixture into mushroom caps.

— Place in a greased shallow baking pan.

— Dot each mushroom with butter

— Bake at 350⁰ for 20 minutes

— Serve sprinkled with chopped parsley

Mushroom Caviar

½ lb. mushrooms, minced
4 Tbls. butter
2 Tbls. minced onion
2 Tbls. lemon juice
1 Tbls. worcestershire sauce
3 Tbls. mayonnaise
½ tsp. salt
dash of pepper

—Sauté mushrooms in butter for about 5 minutes.

—Add onion, sauté for 5 more minutes.

—Remove from heat, cool slightly, drain.

—Add remaining ingredients.

—Mix well.

—Chill and serve with toasted rounds.

Mushrooms Florentine

2 packages frozen chopped spinach
1 tsp. instant chicken bouillon
36 large mushrooms
4 Tbls. butter
¼ tsp. garlic powder
¼ tsp. dry mustard
¼ tsp. seasoned salt
Parmesan cheese, grated

— Clean mushrooms, separate stems and caps.

— Cook spinach as directed, adding chicken bouillon to the water. Drain well.

— Chop mushroom stems and sauté in butter.

— Combine spinach and seasonings.

— Lightly sauté mushroom caps in butter.

— Fill caps with spinach mixture.

— Sprinkle tops with parmesan.

— Bake in shallow dish in a 375⁰ oven for 15 minutes.

— Serve warm.

Mushroom Tidbits

1 eight oz. package cream cheese, softened
1 Tbls. snipped green onions or chives
1 Tbls. butter, softened
1 three oz. can chopped mushrooms, drained
¼ tsp. garlic powder

—Combine all ingredients, mixing well.

—Spread on crackers.

—Sprinkle with paprika.

—Broil 3 to 5 minutes.

—Serve warm.

Mustard Cheese Stuffed Celery

1 three oz. package cream cheese
2 Tbls. mustard
1 large jar (8 oz.) sharp cheese
1 cup finely chopped pecans
2 Tbls. worcestershire sauce
1 tsp. Durkee's dressing
1 stalk celery
paprika

— Combine all ingredients except celery and paprika.

— Blend well.

— Wash celery and cut into 1½" to 2" strips.

— Stuff with cheese mixture.

— Sprinkle with paprika.

Not bad on crackers either.

Roquefort Artichokes

⅓ cup olive oil
⅓ cup white wine vinegar
3 Tbls. crushed roquefort cheese
¼ tsp. basil
¼ tsp. oregano
2 Tbls. chopped parsley
2 Tbls. chopped onion
2 cloves garlic, crushed
salt & pepper to taste
4 cans artichoke hearts, cut in half

— Mix all ingredients - stir well.

— Pour over artichoke hearts which have been drained.

— Refrigerate at least 24 hours.

— Drain, serve with toothpicks.

Spiced Carrot Sticks

5 large carrots (1 lb.)
1 cup white wine vinegar
½ cup orange juice
¼ cup honey
1 Tbls. pickling spices

— Peel carrots and cut into thin 3" long strips or cut into thin slices.

— In medium saucepan, combine vinegar, orange juice, honey and pickling spices.

— Add carrot sticks or slices. Bring to a boil.

— Simmer over medium - low heat 8 - 10 minutes until carrots are "crisp - tender."

— Cool on wire rack for 15 minutes.

— Pour carrots and sauce into a medium sized bowl with a tight fitting lid.

— Cover and refrigerate 6 hours or overnight.

— Drain and serve cold.

Tips on Celery Curls.

Cut stalks of celery into 3 or 4 inch pieces. With sharp knife, make 5 or 6 incisions down stalk, stopping within 1½ inches of end.
Drop pieces in water. Refrigerate for several hours. Split ends will curl back along stalk making an attractive garnish.

Spinach Balls

2 boxes chopped frozen spinach, cooked and drained.
2 cups Pepperidge Farm herb seasoned dressing
1 small onion chopped fine
4 well beaten eggs
¾ cup melted butter
½ cup grated Parmesan cheese
½ tsp. salt
dash of pepper

Preheat oven 375⁰

— Mix all ingredients, chill

— Roll into 1" balls

— Freeze on cookie sheets

— Cook frozen for 20 minutes

53

Stuffed Brussels Sprouts

1 lb. Brussel sprouts
3 oz. softened cream cheese
2 Tbls. chives
½ tsp. worcestershire
salt
fresh ground black pepper
paprika

— Steam Brussels sprouts until tender but not real soft. Cool.

— Hollow out each slightly from the top. (Save center.)

— Mix cream cheese, chives, and worcestershire sauce.

— Chop centers of sprouts, add to cream cheese mixture.

— Salt and pepper to taste.

— Fill each sprout with part of mixture.

— Garnish with paprika and parsley.

Stuffed Cucumbers

4 cucumbers, chilled and peeled
½ cup crumbled feta cheese
1 Tbls. mayonnaise
2 drops worcestershire sauce
1 Tbls. minced parsley

— Cut chilled cucumbers in half, lengthwise and hollow out the center.

— Combine the crumbled feta cheese with the mayonnaise & worcestershire. Mash well.

— Stuff cucumber boats with the cheese mixture, sprinkle tops with parsley.

— Chill.

— Serve with knife to slice off pieces. (Quite different.)

Stuffed Jalapenos

1 can "Jacques Clemente" whole jalapenos.
½ cup shredded cheddar cheese
¼ cup chopped pecans
3 Tbls. mayonnaise

— Drain the jalapenos, cut lengthwise and remove seeds. Rinse and drain on paper towels. Dry thoroughly.

— Mix cheese, nuts, and mayonnaise.

— Fill each jalapeno boat with cheese mixture.

— Refrigerate before serving.

(Men love these!)

Stuffed Snow Peas

1 eight oz. pkg. cream cheese with chives
1 tsp. seasoned salt
48 snow peas

— Soften cream cheese and add salt. Place in pastry bag using leaf tip.

— Wash snow peas, drain and slice open or "unzip" so snow pea pod opens to reveal peas.

— Using pastry tube, pipe cream cheese into the open pods.

— Refrigerate. Serve chilled.

(If you don't have a pastry tube use a small spoon and stuff mixture into pea pods.)

Vegetables Vinaigrette

1 cucumber
3 carrots
½ head cauliflower
½ lb. string beans
1 lb. mushrooms sliced
6 Tbls. tarragon vinegar
½ cup vegetable oil
4 Tbls. olive oil
4 Tbls. lemon juice
1 tsp. sugar
1 Tbls. salt
1 Tbls. dill weed

—Score cucumber and slice ¼ inch thick.

—Slice carrots in sticks or circles.

—Separate cauliflower and clean string beans.

—Combine vinegar, oils, lemon juice, sugar, salt, and dill weed.

—Mix well until blended.

—Pour over vegetables.

—Marinate in refrigerator for up to three days.

Wrapped Celery Chunks

10 4" celery stalks
1 five oz. jar pineapple cream cheese
1 - 2½ oz. pkg. very thinly sliced spiced beef or turkey.

— Fill celery stalks with cream cheese,

— Wrap each filled stalk in a slice of beef or turkey.

— Place seamside down on a small platter.

— Refrigerate at least one hour.

— Cut each stalk into 3 or 4 pieces.
— Secure meat with wooden toothpick if necessary.

NUTS AND NONSENSE

Almond Croquettes

2 Tbls. butter
2 Tbls. flour
1 cup milk
1 cup blanched ground almonds
2 eggs
cracker crumbs
oil for frying

— Make a heavy sauce by cooking butter, flour, and milk.

— Cook until it begins to thicken, stirring constantly.

— Add ground almonds to sauce and mix well. Pour into a flat dish.

— When cool cut into small squares and roll into oblong pieces.

— Beat eggs.

— Dip pieces in eggs then roll in cracker crumbs.

— Fry a few at a time until a delicate brown in deep hot oil.

Basic Party Mix

6 Tbls. butter
4 tsp. worcestershire sauce
1 tsp. seasoned salt
2 cups corn chex
2 cups wheat chex
2 cups rice chex
2 cups thin pretzel sticks
12 oz. mixed nuts

—Melt butter and add worcestershire sauce and salt.

—Place cereal, nuts, and pretzels in a bowl.

—Pour butter mixture over cereals and toss until well coated.

—Place on cookie sheets or 13"x 9"x 2" dish.

—Place in oven at 200^0 for 45 minutes mixing well.

Candied Walnuts or Pecans

⅓ cup sour cream
1 cup sugar
dash salt
1 Tbls. white "Karo" syrup
¼ tsp. vanilla
1 Tbls. butter
2 cups pecans or walnuts

— Mix sour cream, sugar, salt and Karo syrup together in a saucepan.

— Boil, stirring constantly until it forms a soft ball in cold water or $240°$ on a candy thermometer.

— Remove from heat.

— Add vanilla & butter.

— Beat and cool slightly.
  Add nuts.

— Turn out on wax paper and separate.

Chinese Peanuts

1 can Chinese fried noodles
½ lb. Spanish peanuts
1 tsp. butter
½ tsp. accent
½ tsp. salt

— Place peanuts and noodles in a frying pan.

— Add remaining ingredients and heat until butter is melted.

— Stir constantly so nothing burns.

Serve hot or cold.

(Try a pinch of Parmesan)

Curried Nuts

2 cups mixed nuts
½ tsp. curry powder

— Preheat oven to 400⁰.

— Arrange nuts in shallow baking dish.

— Sprinkle with curry powder.

— Roast for 5 - 10 minutes in pre-heated oven.

— Stir occasionally.

Deviled Almonds

1½ cups blanched whole almonds
¼ cup butter
¼ cup salad oil
1 tsp. celery salt
½ tsp. salt
½ tsp. chili powder
1/8 tsp. cayenne pepper

— Combine butter and oil in skillet.

— Add almonds.

— Cook and stir over medium heat until golden.

— Remove almonds and drain on paper towels.

— Sprinkle spices over almonds while hot.

— Stir to coat.

Hot Herbed Pretzels

2 Tbls. butter
½ tsp. crumbled tarragon
2 tsps. parsley flakes
¼ tsp. onion powder
2 cups pretzels

— Place butter in a 2-quart utility dish. Heat in radar-range until butter is melted. (30 - 40 seconds.)

— Blend in seasonings.

— Add pretzels to toss & coat.

— Heat in radar range for 1½ minutes or until heated through. (Stir half-way through cooking time.)

Great for TV football watchers!

Hot Nut Crackers

½ cup butter
1 cup pre-sifted flour
½ lb. mild Cheddar cheese, shredded
¼ tsp. salt
½ tsp. red pepper
4 Tbls. ice water
48 pecan halves

—Cream butter until fluffy. Combine flour, cheese, salt and pepper. Slowly add this to butter along with water to make a firm dough. Chill.

—Preheat oven to 350°. Grease baking sheet.

—Roll out dough thinly on lightly floured board.

—Cut into rounds with a small biscuit cutter.

—Place pecan half on each round; fold over like tiny turnovers and seal edges with a fork.

—Sprinkle with paprika.

—Bake in a preheated oven for 15 minutes or until crisp.

Incredible Nut Mix

1 Box white raisins
1 16 oz. bag salted Redskin peanuts
1 8 oz. box chopped sugared dates
1 small bag unsalted sunflower seeds
16 ozs. pecan halves
12 ozs. cashews, salted
12 ozs. whole almonds
8 ozs. walnut pieces

— Mix all together.

— This recipe makes a lot.

— Give as gifts packed in pretty tins.

— A great hostess gift!

Oyster Cracker Snacks
(for microwaves)

1 cup butter
1½ tsps. celery salt
1½ tsps. garlic salt
1½ tsps. onion salt
1 tsp. paprika
½ cup Parmesan cheese (grated)
1 10 oz. package oyster crackers (6 cups)

— Place butter in a 2 quart utility dish. Heat in radar-range for 1 minute or until butter is melted.

— Blend in seasonings and cheese.

— Stir in crackers. Toss until well coated.

— Heat in a radar-range for 3 to 3½ minutes until heated throughout. Stir halfway through cooking time.

— Cool and store in plastic bag or airtight container.

Parmesan-Glazed Walnuts

1½ cup walnut halves
1 Tbls. butter
¼ tsp. hickory-smoked salt
¼ tsp. salt
¼ cup Parmesan cheese

—Heat oven to 350⁰.

—Spread walnuts in shallow baking pan; toast in oven for 10 minutes.

—Stir together butter and salts. Toss lightly in walnuts.

—Sprinkle cheese on top. Stir.

—Return to oven and heat 3 - 4 minutes until cheese melts.

Roasted Pumpkin Seeds

2 cups pumpkin seeds
1½ Tbls. melted butter
1¼ tsp. salt

— Preheat oven to 250⁰.

— Combine pumpkin seeds and salt.

— Mix well - spread in shallow pan with melted butter.

— Roast in pre-heated oven for 30 - 40 minutes or until browned and crisp, stirring often to brown evenly

Roasted Sunflower Seeds

2 cups seeds
Vegetable oil
Salt

— Spread sunflower seeds on large baking sheet and toast in preheated 300⁰ oven for 10 minutes.

— Drizzle slightly with oil, sprinkle with salt and turn.

— Continue to toast, stirring often, for 30 minutes more until crisp as desired.

Roquefort Pecans or Walnuts

1 3 oz. pkg. Roquefort or Blue cheese
1 3 oz. pkg. cream cheese
¾ lb. pecan or walnut halves

— Crumble Roquefort or Blue cheese.

— Beat cheese into cream cheese until fluffy

— Spread on flat side of a nut half; put flat side
  of another nut on top.

— Press together.

— Chill.

Cute!

Seeded Crackers

24 saltines, rich round crackers, crisp rye
    wafers or other crackers
1 stick butter, melted

— Brush top side of crackers with melted butter.

— Place on baking sheet.

— Sprinkle with:
        onion or garlic powder
    or - caraway seeds
    or - celery seeds
    or - dill weed
    or - poppy seeds
    or - sesame seeds

— Heat on baking sheet at 350^0 for 5 minutes or
until crisp and hot.

Smoked Almonds

2 cups unblanched almonds
½ cup liquid smoke
½ stick butter

—Soak almonds in liquid smoke for 20 minutes.

—Drain well.

—Spread almonds on a baking sheet and toast slowly in a 250⁰ oven about 1 hour or until crisp.

—While nuts are hot, brush with melted butter.

—Salt to taste.

—Drain on paper towels.

Spiced Cocktail Nuts

¼ cup butter
1 Tbls. Worcestershire sauce
½ tsp. bottled hot pepper sauce
1 Tbls. salad seasoning
1 tsp. salt
½ tsp. garlic salt
¼ tsp. pepper
1 lb. walnut halves, whole almonds or whole
   filberts

—In a 12" skillet with a tight-fitting lid, combine butter, Worcestershire, pepper sauce, salad seasoning, salt, garlic salt and pepper.

—Stir until well blended.

—Add nuts - toss to coat.

—Cook, covered, over low heat for 20 minutes, stirring occasionally.

—Cool on paper towels.

—Store in airtight containers.

Spiced Pecans

2 cups pecan halves
1½ Tbls. butter, melted
1 tsp. salt
2 tsp. soy sauce
1/8 tsp. tabasco

— Preheat oven to 300⁰

— In 8" x 9" cake pan combine pecans with melted butter.

— Toast in oven for 25 minutes, stirring occasionally.

— Add salt, soy sauce and tabasco.

— Toss well to coat pecans.

Serve hot or cold.

Sugared Nuts

1 lb. pecan halves, walnut halves, or almond
  halves or wholes
1 Tbls. water
1 egg white
½ cup sugar
½ tsp. salt
½ tsp. cinnamon
Dash of freshly grated nutmeg

—Preheat oven to 225°.

—Beat eggwhite with 1 Tbls. water.

—Coat nuts with egg and water mixture.

—Mix sugar, salt, cinnamon, and nutmeg.

—Roll nuts in sugar mixture.

—Spread nuts on cookie sheet.

—Cook one hour, stirring every 15 minutes.

—Cool.

—Store in refrigerator.

Sugar Glazed Walnuts
(This recipe is for those of you who have microwave ovens!)

½ cup butter
1 cup brown sugar
1 tsp. cinnamon
1 lb. walnut halves

—Melt butter in 1½ quart casserole for one minute in microwave.

—Stir in sugar and cinnamon. Cook in microwave for 2 minutes. Mix well.

—Add nuts. Stir to coat and cook 3-5 minutes in microwave.

—Spread out onto wax paper and cool slightly.

Serve warm or cold.

Teriyaki Toasted Nuts
(Use unsalted nuts if you prefer a less salty snack!)

2 cups mixed nuts
2 Tbls. butter
1 Tbl. soy sauce
½ tsp. ground ginger
¼ tsp. garlic salt
1 tsp. lemon juice

—Preheat oven to 325⁰ F.

—Spread nuts on a large ungreased baking sheet with raised sides.

—Roast nuts 5-10 minutes until lightly brown.

—In a small skillet, melt butter.

—Stir in soy sauce, ginger, garlic salt and lemon juice; brush over toasted nuts.

—Roast 5 minutes longer until golden brown.

The Ol' Time Favorite, Nuts & Bolts

1 package cherrios
1 package each;
  Rice, Wheat &
  Corn Chex
1 package KIX (plain)
1 package stick type
  pretzels
1 lb. mixed nuts
2 cans pumpkin seeds

1 lb. butter
¾ cup bacon grease
½ bottle (small) tabasco
2 cloves garlic, smashed
2 Tbls. Worcestershire
2 tsps. picapepper sauce
2 tsps. celery salt
1 tsp. chili powder
1 tsp. curry power

— Melt butter, add bacon grease, sauces, and spices.

— Pour over mixture in a very large bowl or better yet, both parts of a large turkey roaster.

— Mix with hands.

— Cook at 200° for an hour, stirring occasionally.

Makes great party gifts!

Toasted Butter Pecans

4 cups pecans
1 Tbls. seasoned salt
¼ cup butter

— Place pecans in 1½ quart casserole.

— Sprinkle with seasoned salt.

— Cut butter and arrange evenly over the top of
the pecans.

— Cook in microwave for 5-6 minutes or in con-
ventional oven at 350⁰ for 12-15 minutes.

— Stir to distribute butter.

Serve warm or cold.

Toasted Pecans

1 egg white, beaten until foamy, not stiff
½ tsp. salt
½ tsp. cloves
½ tsp. cinnamon
½ tsp. allspice
½ cup sugar
3 cups pecan halves

— Place egg white, which is foamy, into a bowl.

— Add spices and sugar, mix thoroughly.

— Roll pecan halves in egg white and spice mixture until well coated.

— Bake at 250⁰ for 1 hour on buttered cookie sheet, stirring occasionally.

Walnut Snack

1 cup walnut halves
2 tsp. butter
1 tsp. onion salt

—Place walnuts in shallow pan. Dot with butter.

—Heat in 350⁰ oven for 15 minutes, stirring occasionally.

—Remove from oven; sprinkle with onion salt.

—Cool on paper towels.

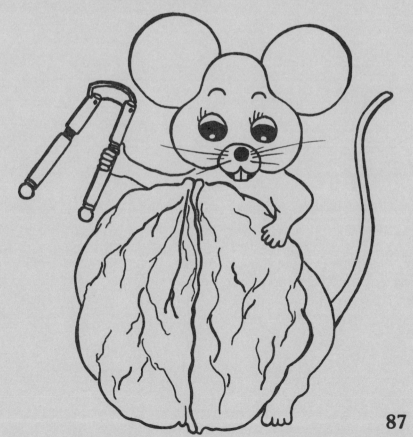

CHEESE THINGS

A-1 Cheese Ball

1 8 oz. package cream cheese
⅓ stick butter, softened
3 Tbls. A-1 sauce
1 Tbls. lemon juice
1 tsp. Worcestershire sauce
1 cup chopped pecans

— Combine all ingredients except pecans.

— Blend well.

— Chill.

— Roll into ball.

— Roll ball into pecans, coating well.

Serve with crackers.

(This is an interesting combination of ingredients. So quick and so-o-o good!)

Almond or Pistachio Cheese Log

1 cup shredded Cheddar cheese
1 16 oz. package cream cheese, softened
2 tsp. prepared mustard
½ cup slivered almonds or chopped
  pistacho nuts

— Cream cheeses with the mustard.

— On waxed paper, shape into an 8 inch long
  roll.

— Roll in nuts.

— Wrap in plastic.

— Chill.

— Let it get to room temperature before serving.

Cheese Crispies
(A different version of the cheese wafer!)

½ lb. sharp Cheddar cheese, grated
3 Tbls. butter
¾ cup flour
½ tsp. celery powder
2 tsp. Worcestershire sauce
½ tsp. salt
¼ tsp. white pepper
Grated Parmesan cheese
paprika

— Soften butter in a bowl.

— Add cheese, flour, celery powder, Worcestershire sauce, salt, and white pepper.

— Mix well (makes a very stiff dough).

— Divide dough in half - form 2 rolls 1½ inches in diameter.

— Wrap up and refrigerate until firm enough to slice.

— Slice ¼ inch wafers and arrange on lightly greased cookie sheets.

— Sprinkle with Parmesan and paprika.

— Bake at 450° for 8-10 minutes until puffed and golden brown.

— Serve at room temperature.

Cheese Log

1½ lbs. Longhorn cheese, grated
1 8 oz. package Philadelphia creamed cheese
½ cup finely chopped pecans
3 cloves garlic, crushed, or
    ¾ tsp. garlic powder
Chili powder

— Grate cheese.

— Soften cream cheese.

— Add pecans and garlic.

— Sprinkle chili powder on wax paper and shape
  cheese mixture into 3 square rolls.

— Cover with chili powder on all sides.

— Chill overnight.

Makes 3 long rolls.

Serve with crackers.

Cheese Medley

1 cup shredded Swiss cheese (4 oz.)
1 cup shredded American cheese (4 oz.)
1 3 oz. package cream cheese, softened
¼ cup mayonnaise
1 tsp. Worcestershire sauce
2 Tbls. chopped pimiento
1 tsp. onion powder
¼ tsp. bottled hot pepper sauce
½ cup crushed potato chips
1½ tsp. grated Parmesan cheese

— Bring Swiss and American cheeses to room temperature.

— In a small mixing bowl beat together the cream cheese and mayonnaise with mixer.

— Stir in Swiss and American cheeses.

— Add pimiento, Worcestershire, onion powder and pepper sauce.

— Chill for at least one hour.

— Shape into a ball.

— Combine potato chips and Parmesan cheese.

— Roll ball into mixture, coating well.

— Wrap in clear plastic wrap.

— Refrigerate until firm.

Serve with assorted crackers.

Cheese Mousse

1½ packages unflavored gelatin
¼ cup cold water
2 cups sour cream
2 tsps. Italian salad dressing package mix
¼ cup crumbled Bleu cheese
1 8 oz. carton small curd cottage cheese

— Soften gelatin in cold water.

— Place over boiling water and stir until the gelatin is dissolved.

— Stir gelatin into the sour cream.

— Add the salad dressing mix, Bleu cheese, and cottage cheese.

— Beat with electric mixer until well blended.

— Pour into 3½ cup ring mold.

— Chill until it is firm.

— Unmold.

— Garnish

Serve with crackers.

Cheese Spread

2 sticks butter, softened
¼ lb. sharp Cheddar cheese, grated
¼ lb. grated Romano cheese
1 tsp. Worcestershire sauce
Scant ¼ tsp. garlic powder
½ tsp. paprika
Sourdough French bread

— Let cheese get to room temperature.

— Combine soft butter with cheeses in mixer bowl.

— Whip slowly until mixture is fluffy.

— Spread on French bread that has been sliced and toast under broiler.

Cheese Straws

¼ lb. butter
2 cups flour
1 lb. Cheddar cheese
¼ tsp. cayenne pepper
½ tsp. salt

— Preheat oven to 400°

— Cream butter.

— Add flour, cayenne, cheese, and salt.

— Roll out onto a floured surface.

— Cut into 4 - 5 inch strips about 3/8 inch to 1/2 inch wide.

— Place on greased cookie sheet.

— Bake 6 minutes or until golden brown.

Easy and Tasty.

Chile con Queso

1 cup chopped drained canned tomatoes
2 Tbls. butter
2 Tbls. flour
1 cup light cream
½ tsp. finely chopped garlic
½ tsp. salt
4 oz. can green chilies - not jalapenos -
    drained, seeded, skinned and chopped
2 cups (½ lb.) grated Monterey Jack

— In heavy saucepan melt butter.

— When foam subsides, add flour and mix well.

— Stir constantly with wire whisk, pour in cream slowly.

— Cook till sauce comes to a boil, thickens, and is smooth.

— Reduce heat, cook 2 minutes - set aside.

— Combine tomatoes, garlic, and salt in heavy skillet.

— Heat until mixture is thick enough to hold shape.

— Reduce heat and add cream sauce and chiles.

— Add cheese, but do not let mixture come to a boil.

— When cheese melts, transfer to a chafing dish.

Serve with tortilla chips.

Fondue of Brie

1½ to 2 lb. round of Brie cheese
1 cup toasted almond slices
Melba toast or sliced hard rolls

—One hour before serving, place Brie, bottom up, on a flameproof platter.

—After 30 minutes, remove skin or the thin layer of crust.

—Place under a pre-heated broiler until surface bubbles.

—Garnish with toasted almonds.

—Serve hot, surrounded with the toast or roll slices.

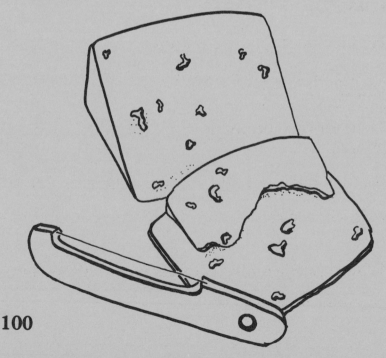

Garlic Cheese Ball

2 cups grated Monterey Jack
1 3 oz. package cream cheese
1 cup mayonnaise
1 clove garlic, chopped
1 small onion, finely chopped
1 tsp. Worcestershire sauce
1 tsp. salt
½ tsp. paprika
Parsley flakes

—Combine cheeses, mayonnaise, garlic, onion, Worcestershire sauce, salt, and paprika.

—Mix well.

—Form into a ball.

—Roll in parsley flakes.

—Chill.

Serve with crackers.

Lincoln Cheese & Beef Log

½ lb. or 8 oz. cream cheese
¼ cup grated Swiss cheese
¼ cup coarsely chopped dried beef
2 tsps. prepared horseradish
1 Tbl. chopped parsley

— Blend together cream cheese, Swiss cheese and horseradish, adding a few drops of cream or milk if the the mixture seems too stiff.

— Chill mixture for one hour.

— Form into one long roll about 1½ inches in diameter.

— Sprinkle dried beef and parsley on waxed paper and roll cheese around until the log is covered.

— Chill overnight to blend flavors.

Serve with crackers.

Miniature Cream Puffs

½ cup water
¼ cup butter
1/8 tsp. salt
½ cup flour
¼ cup finely grated Cheddar cheese optional
2 eggs

—Combine water and butter in a saucepan.

—Add salt and flour all at once; stir quickly until mixture forms a ball.

—Remove from heat.

—Add cheese if desired.

—Beat in one egg at a time, beating well until mixture is like velvet.

—Refrigerate mixture for 1 hour.

—Place 1 scant teaspoonful on a lightly greased cookie sheet; mound with tip of spoon.

—Bake in a 400⁰ oven for 15 - 18 minutes until puffed and golden brown.

—Split cream puffs in half and fill with desired filling.

Cream Cheese and Olive Filling

1 8 oz. package cream cheese
½ tsp. instant chicken boullion
1 Tbl. minced onion
½ cup chopped ripe olives
2 Tbls. mayonnaise

— Combine all ingredients.

— Mix well.

— Fill puffs.

Cucumber Filling

1 cup chopped cucumber
1 3 oz. package cream cheese, softened
½ tsp. grated onion
½ tsp. salt
Dash of pepper
2 to 3 Tbls. mayonnaise

—Combine all ingredients.

—Mix well.

—Fill puffs.

Meat Fillings for Puffs

1½ cup chopped cooked chicken, shrimp or
      crabmeat
2 Tbls. minced celery or water chestnuts
1 tsp. minced onion
      Seasoned salt to taste
3 to 4 Tbls. mayonnaise

— Combine all ingredients.

— Mix well.

— Fill puffs.

No Trump Cheese Wafers

2¼ cup sifted flour
1 tsp. salt
2 cups grated sharp cheddar cheese
¼ cup dry sherry
1 cup shortening
Sprinkle of cayenne

— Combine flour, salt, and cayenne.

— Cut in the shortening.

— Add cheese and mix with a fork.

— Sprinkle sherry over the surface and mix until stiff dough is formed.

— Roll about 1/8 inch thick on lightly floured board and cut with any desired small cutter.

— Prick each one with fork.

— Top with a small pecan half or olive slice.

— Bake on greased baking sheets at 300⁰ for 15-18 minutes until baked through but not brown.

— Cool on wire racks and store in tightly covered tin.

Great with mixed drinks.

Party Cheese Spread

1 cup cheddar cheese spread
1 3 oz. package cream cheese
1 cup small curd cottage cheese
¼ cup orange liqueur
½ cup chopped walnuts

— Mix cheeses together until smooth.

— Add liqueur and nuts.

— Shape into a ball.

— Chill for several hours.

— Serve at room temperature with crackers.

Rolled Cheese Ball

1 3 oz. package cream cheese
8 ozs. Gorgonzola or blue cheese
¼ cup heavy cream
1 Tbls. finely chopped parsley
Dash of Worcestershire sauce
1 cup finely chopped walnuts

— Combine cheeses, cream, parsley, and Worcestershire sauce.

— Chill until easy enough to form into a ball.

— Roll in walnuts.

— Chill.

— Serve with crackers.

Roquefort Tomatoes

2 dozen cherry tomatoes
1/2 cup Roquefort cheese
1 Tbls. heavy cream
1/8 tsp. celery salt
2 oz. black caviar
2 dozen toast rounds

— Slice off tops of tomatoes.

— Gently squeeze out seeds and juice.

— Cream cheese with the heavy cream and celery salt.

— Stuff 1 tsp. of this mixture into each tomato.

— Top each tomato with a dollop of black caviar.

— Place on toast rounds.

— Chill before serving

Sesame Cheese Sticks

1 lb. sharp cheddar cheese, grated.
1 stick butter, creamed.
1/2 cup toasted sesame seeds
2 cups flour
1/2 tsp. salt
1/2 tsp. cayenne
1/9 tsp. fresh grated nutmeg

— Mix together flour, salt, cayenne and nutmeg.

— Cream butter, add cheddar cheese

— Add flour mixture.

— Now add sesame seeds

— Make into a dough.

— Pinch off pieces of dough and roll with your hand into long pencil shapes, ¼ inch in diameter and 4-6 inches long.

— If dough is too warm, refrigerate. This makes it easier to handle.

— Place cheese sticks on ungreased cookie sheets, 1 inch apart.

— Bake at 350⁰ for 15 minutes or until puffed and golden. (Not brown.)

— Serve warm or at room temperature.

Sesame Made Simple

1 8 oz. package cream cheese, chilled
½ cup toasted sesame seeds

—Cut cream cheese into ½ inch cubes.

—Roll in toasted sesame seeds

—Chill.

—Serve with crackers

So simple and so quick!

Thank Goodness for Cream Cheese!

Sherried Cheese

1 8 oz. package cream cheese, softened.
½ 10½ oz. can beef consomme
1 Tbls. sherry
½ cucumber, drained and minced

—Mix together all ingredients well.

—Chill and serve with crackers

Sherry Wine Cheese Spread

4 cups shredded natural cheddar cheese (16 oz.)
½ cup crumbled blue cheese (2 oz.)
¼ cup butter, softened
½ cup dry sherry
2 tsps. dry mustard
Dash cayenne pepper

—In bowl combine cheese, butter, sherry, mustard, and cayenne.

—Beat until well blended.

—Pack into lightly oiled 3 cup mold.

—Cover tighly.

—Chill.

—Unmold and let stand at room temperature.

—Garnish with parsley or whatever looks pretty.

—Serve with sliced fruit and crackers.

Trés Cream Cheese

3 small packages (3 oz.) cream cheese
3 Tbls. toasted sesame seeds
3 Tbls. chopped chives
2-3 Tlbs. picante sauce (Paces is good!)

— Leave cream cheese blocks whole.

— Coat one block with sesame seeds

— Coat one block with chives

— Pour picante sauce over 1 block

— Serve all three blocks of cheese together at
 room temperature.

— Serve with crackers

Watercress Cheese Spread

2 3 oz. packages cream cheese with
chives, softened
¼ cup butter, softened
1 Tbl. onion
1 Tbl. mayonnaise
1 bunch watercress, minced

—Blend cheese with butter, onion, and mayonnaise until smooth.

—Blend in watercress.

—Serve with toast rounds.

PORK PICK-EM-UPS

Bacon and Crackers

Escort or Waverly crakers
Bacon Strips
Parmesan cheese

— Cover crackers with Parmesan cheese.

— Wrap bacon strips around crackers.

— Bake on wire racks for one hour - 300°-325°.

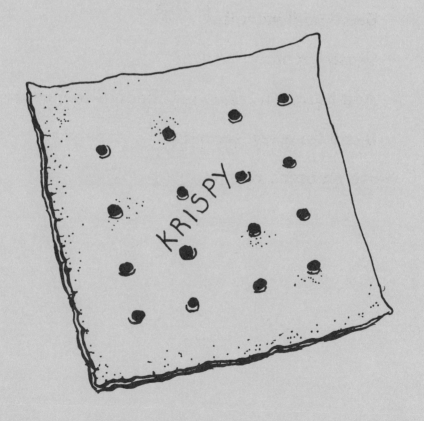

Bacon and Tomato Spread

3 strips bacon
1 small tomato, peeled and quartered
1 tsp. prepared mustard
1 3 oz. package cream cheese
¼ tsp. celery salt
½ cup blanched, chopped almonds

—Fry bacon until crisp, drain well.

—Put tomato, mustard, cream cheese and celery salt into blender.

—Blend until smooth.

—Crush bacon.

—Add bacon and chopped almonds to mixture.

—Blend for a few seconds.

Serve on bread rounds.

Bacon Poles
(for microwaves)

10 strips bacon; cut bacon strips in half, lengthwise, making 2 long thin strips
20 long thin garlic breadsticks, or sesame breadsticks

—Wrap one strip of bacon in a spiral (barber pole fashion) around each breadstick.

—Place 2 paper towels in bottom of a 13 x 9 x 2 inch glass dish.

—Distribute wrapped bread sticks so they do not touch each other.

—Cover with a paper towel.

—Microwave 10 - 13 minutes, rotating dish ½ turn every five minutes until the bacon is cooked.

Bacon Wrapped Artichoke Hearts

2 cans (14 oz.) Artichoke hearts
½ lb. thin-sliced bacon cut in half

—Cut Artichoke hearts in half.

—Wrap ½ bacon strip around the Artichoke heart and secure it with a toothpick.

—Place on baking sheet and bake at 400° for 8 -10 minutes until the bacon is crisp.

—Drain.

—Serve warm.

Bacon-wrapped Water Chestnuts

2 cans <u>La Choy</u> whole water chestnuts
1 small bottle soy sauce
Granulated sugar
1 lb. thin-sliced bacon

— Drain chestnuts and pour soy sauce completely over them. Let them soak for at least two hours.

— Roll soaked water chestnuts in white granulated sugar.

— Wrap each water chestnut in ½ slice of bacon.

— Secure with toothpick.

— Arrange water chestnuts on a broiling pan.

— Broil until one side is golden brown.

— Turn over and watch closely.

— Serve warm.

Deviled Ham Spread

2 small cans (4½ oz.) deviled ham
½ cup diced celery
1 tsp. chopped pimiento
1 tsp. minced onion, or better yet, shallots
⅓ cup mayonnaise

— Mix all of the above ingredients together and chill.

— Use as a spread or on crackers or corn chips.

— Garnish with sliced ripe or green stuffed olives.

Ham Balls

2 cups ground ham
3 hardboiled eggs
1 Tbl. minced onion
½ tsp. tabasco
¼ cup Parmesan or
    ½ tsp. seasoned salt
Chopped almonds
½ cup melted butter

—Mix everything together except for almonds and butter.

—Make into 1 tsp. small balls.

—Dip balls into the melted butter.

—Roll each ball in chopped almonds.

—Chill and serve.

Sausage Balls

1 lb. Coon brand sharp Cheddar cheese
1 lb. hot ground sausage
3 cups Bisquick

— Grate cheese.

— Add cheese to crumbled raw sausage and Bisquick.

— Roll into 1 inch balls.

— Bake in a 350^0 oven for 20 minutes or until golden brown.

This recipe makes Mass Quantities.

DIPS A LA CARTE

Basic Dippers

Asparagus Spears
Artichokes or pickled Artichoke hearts
Broccoli spears
Baby Brussel sprouts
Black olives
Carrot sticks
Celery sticks
Cucumber slices or spears
Cabbage, purple leaves
Cauliflowerets
Cherry peppers
Cherry tomatoes
Green onions
Green pepper strips
Kohlrabi slices
Raw mushrooms
Radishes
Romaine lettuce
Sliced yellow and Zucchini squash
Snow peas
Stemmed green beans
Scallions
Turnip slices

Artichoke Dip

1 can (1 pound) Artichoke hearts, drained
⅓ cup mayonnaise
1 Tbl. chopped onion
Juice of ½ lemon
Salt, pepper, and a dash of cayenne

— Chop Artichoke hearts until fine but lumpy.

— Add other ingredients.

— Stir well.

— Chill.

Serve with chips or veggie dippers.

Simple but so good!

Avocado Dip with Red & Black Caviar

1 large ripe avocado
¼ cup sour cream
2 Tbls. lime juice
1/8 tsp. salt
2 Tbls. each black and red caviar

— Split avocado in half, lengthwise, remove pit and carefully scoop out the pulp, preserving the shells.

— Mash pulp and add the sour cream, lime juice and salt until blended.

— Spoon into each shell.

— With the back of a spoon, make a cavity in center of each mound of avocado.

— Fill hollow of one with black caviar, fill the other with red caviar.

— Chill.

— Serve with chips or crackers.

Avocado-Pistachio Cream Dip

2 ripe avocados, quartered
¼ cup lime or lemon juice
½ cup confectioners sugar
½ cup roasted, shelled pistachio nuts
2 Tbls. Creme de Cocoa
1 cup heavy cream, whipped
    (Lime slices for garnish)

—Blend avocados, lime juice, sugar, pistachio nuts (chopped) and Creme de Cocoa until smooth.

—Fold in whipped cream.

—Spoon into pretty crystal or silver serving deep dish.

—Garnish.

—Serve with tiny crackers or fruit bites.

Bacon Dip

1 8 oz. package cream cheese, softened
Milk
1 tsp. grated onion
2 Tbls. minced bell pepper
Salt and pepper
5 slices bacon, cooked until crisp,
     drained and crumbled
Paprika

—Mash cheese with a fork.

—Add milk, 1 Tbl. at a time, mixing well until
  the mixture is a good dippng consistency.

—Add onion, bell pepper, salt, and pepper to
  taste.

—Add the crumbled bacon, mixing well.

—Sprinkle with paprika.

—Serve at room temperature.

—Serve with crackers.

Beef and Cheese Dip

2 lbs. Velveeta cheese
1 large tomato, chopped
1 large can chili-no beans
     (14½ to 19½ oz. size)
2 cloves garlic, pressed
1 medium onion, minced
1 Tbls. Worcestershire sauce

— Melt cheese in top of double boiler.

— Add remaining ingredients.

— Keep warm.

— Serve with tortilla chips.

Blue Tuna Dip

1 6½ oz. can tuna, drained
1 cup small curd cottage cheese
¼ cup crumbled Bleu cheese
1 tsp. Worcestershire sauce
¼ cup finely chopped walnuts
1 Tbls. parsley flakes

— Combine tuna, cheeses, and Worcestershire sauce in blender. Blend for 1 minute.

— Add walnuts and parsley.

— Mix together.

— Refrigerate.

— Serve with all sorts of dippers.

Brunswick Stew Dip

1 cup cream style corn
1 cup cooked baby lima beans
2 medium tomatoes, peeled and chopped
1 green bell pepper, diced
1 cup cooked chicken meat, diced
1 cup tomato sauce
1½ cups sour cream
1 medium onion, chopped
½ tsp. celery powder
½ tsp. salt
¼ tsp. pepper

—Combine all ingredients.

—Stir thoroughly.

—Chill.

—Serve cold with chips.

Chestnut Dip

16 ounces plain yogurt
1 8 oz. can water chestnuts, drained
   and chopped
2 Tbls. snipped green onions
1 Tbls. beef-flavored instant bouillon
2 Tbls. snipped parsley
½ tsp. Worcestershire sauce
¼ tsp. garlic powder
Dash of Tabasco

—Combine all ingredients.

—Chill

—Stir before serving.

—Serve with assorted fresh vegetables.

Chili-Cheese Dip

1 small can (15 oz.) tamales (Ellis)
1 15 ounce can chili, no beans
1 pound Velveeta cheese

— Chop tamales.

— Place cheese in a fondue pot or chafing dish. Melt cheese.

— Add tamales and the can of chili.

— Warm.

— Serve with Doritos or tortilla chips.

Excellent and easy.

Chili con Queso

1 lb. box Old English Cheese (Kraft)
1 large can evaporated milk
1 large onion, chopped fine
¼ cup bacon drippings
1 4 oz. can pickled whole jalapeno
    peppers, drained and chopped
½ tsp. tabasco

—Sauté onions in bacon drippings.

—Add jalapenos.

—Put remaining ingredients in top of double boiler.

—Add everything together.

—Serve warm.

—Serve with tortilla chips.

Crab Creole Dip

¾ cup crabmeat
2 Tbls. minced onion
Juice of ½ lemon
2 Tbls. tomato paste
½ tsp. cayenne pepper
¼ tsp. ground celery seed
1 cup sour cream
1 jalapeno pepper

— Mix everything together except for the sour cream and the pepper.

— Fold in the sour cream.

— Put in serving dish and place the jalapeno pepper in the center of the dip for decoration.

— For a more festive look, add a little dried bell pepper and pimiento to the top.

Creamy Egg Dip

4 hard boiled eggs, chopped
1 8 oz. package creamed cottage cheese
¾ cup mayonnaise
4 green onions, snipped
Salt and pepper to taste

— Combine all ingredients, mixing well.

— Chill several hours.

— Serve with seasoned crackers.

Cucumber Dip

1 large cucumber, peeled and finely minced
    in food processor
1 8 oz. package cream cheese
¼ cup finely chopped green onion
1 Tbl. finely chopped pimiento
1 tsp. seasoned salt

— Mix all ingredients together.

— Chill.

— Serve with crackers.

Cucumber Chile Dip

1 large cucumber
½ tsp. salt
1 small package (3 oz.) cream cheese
2 Tbls. sour cream
2 Tbls. seeded and chopped green chiles

—Peel and mince the cucumber. Mix with salt and chill one hour to release liquid.

—Blend cream cheese with the sour cream until smooth.

—Drain liquid from cucumber.

—Combine cucumber and creamed cheese mixture.

—Stir in chiles.

—Salt to taste.

—Cover and chill.

Great with Veggie Dippers.

Curry Dip

½ cup sour cream
3 Tbls. mayonnaise
½ tsp. curry powder, (or to taste)
1/8 tsp. cayenne
1 Tbls. catsup
¼ tsp. Worcestershire sauce
Dash of salt
1 clove garlic, minced

—Stir together the sour cream, mayonnaise, curry powder, cayenne, catsup, Worcestershire, salt, and garlic.

—Blend well.

—Refrigerate at least 4 hours to let flavors mellow together.

—Stir before serving.

Serve with Veggie Dippers! ie   Dippers!

Deviled Egg Dip

¼ cup mayonnaise
1 3 oz. package cream cheese, room
    temperature
1 Tbl. milk
1 tsp. prepared mustard
¼ tsp. salt
1/8 tsp. pepper
¼ tsp. prepared horseradish
1 tsp. chopped chives
4 hard cooked eggs, finely chopped

—In a medium bowl, beat mayonnaise, cream
  cheese and milk until smooth.

—Stir in mustard, salt, pepper, horseradish,
  chives, and hard cooked eggs.

—Spoon into a small serving dish.

Serve with crackers or raw vegetables.

Deviled Ham Dip

1 jar pimiento cheese spread
½ cup mayonnaise
2 Tbls. deviled ham
1 tsp. grated onions

— Have all ingredients at room temperature.

— Blend together with an electric mixer or with a
  fork.

— Serve with potato chips or veggie dippers.

Easy Caviar Dip

¾ cup sour cream
4 oz. red caviar

—Blend sour cream and caviar together.

—Chill.

—Serve with crackers.

Eggplant Caviar

1 eggplant, medium size
½ cup finely chopped onion
1 clove garlic, crushed
1 tomato, peeled, seeded, and chopped fine
3 Tbls. olive oil
2 Tbls. vinegar
1 tsp. sugar
Salt and pepper
4 Tbls. parsley, chopped

— Peel and cook chunked eggplant until tender.

— Chop fine after cooking.

— Drain and mix with onion, garlic, tomato, oil,
   vinegar, and sugar.

— Season with salt and pepper.

— Cover with parsley and chill for hours.

— Serve with dark bread.

Ginger Dip

½ cup mayonnaise
½ cup dairy sour cream
1 Tbls. finely chopped onion
2 Tbls. crushed parsley
2 Tbls. finely chopped canned water chestnuts
1 Tbl. finely chopped candied ginger
1 clove garlic, minced
1½ tsps. soy sauce

—Combine mayonnaise and sour cream.

—Stir in the remaining ingredients.

—Chill

Serve with chips or sesame crackers.

Green Chile Cheese Dip

1 can (4 oz.) diced green chiles
1 cup sour cream
½ cup finely chopped onion
1 8 oz. package cream cheese, softened
Half and half, 1 tsp at a time

— Add chiles, sour cream, and onion to the cream cheese.

— Beat with mixer until well blended.

— Add enough half and half to get a good dipping consistency.

— Cover and refrigerate for several hours to blend flavors.

— Serve with tortilla chips.

Green Goddess Dip

1 clove garlic
¼ cup coarsely chopped parsley
¼ cup chopped green onion
¼ cup chopped watercress
½ tsp. onion salt
1 tsp. tarragon leaves
1 tsp. anchovy paste
2 tsps. lemon juice
½ cup mayonnaise
½ cup sour cream

— Put garlic, parsley, green onion, watercress, onion salt, tarragon, anchovy paste, and lemon juice in blender.

— Blend until puréed.

— Stir in mayonnaise and sour cream until smooth.

— Chill.

— Serve with veggies.

Guacamole I

2 cups of diced avocadoes
Juice of 2 lemons
2 Tbls. grated onion
3 Tbls. Paces picante sauce
4 drops tabasco sauce
2 small tomatoes, diced
Salt and pepper to taste

Blend all of the ingredients together.

—Chill.

—Serve with tortilla chips.

(A tip from Helen Corbitt: if you put the pit of the avocado in the center of the dip while storing in the refrigerator, this will aid in the dip not turning color. Remove pit when serving.)

Guacamole II

1 avocado (smashed)
½ tomato (chopped)
Garlic powder to taste
2 green onions, chopped fine
Picante sauce or Louisiana Hot Sauce
Juice of ¼ lemon
Salt to taste

— Smash avocado.

— Add tomato, chopped onions, and lemon juice.

— Add picante sauce, a tsp. at a time to taste.

— Season with garlic powder and salt to taste.

156

Herby Curry Dip

1 cup mayonnaise
½ cup sour cream
1 tsp. fines herbes, crushed
¼ tsp. salt
1/8 tsp. curry powder
1 Tbl. crushed parsley
1 Tbl. grated onion
1½ tsp. lemon juice
½ tsp. Worcestershire sauce
2 tsps. capers, drained

—Mix all ingredients together.

—Chill.

—Serve with chips or veggie dippers.

Horseradish Dip

1 8 oz. package cream cheese
2 Tbls. milk
2 Tbls. prepared horseradish
¼ tsp. Worcestershire sauce
Dash of salt
Paprika

— Combine cream cheese and milk, blending until smooth.

— Add horseradish, Worcestershire sauce and salt. Mix well.

— Sprinkle with paprika.

Serve with chips or veggie dippers!

Hot Broccoli Dip

3 stalks celery, chopped finely
½ white onion, finely chopped
1 can mushroom, chopped
1 package frozen chopped broccoli
1 can cream of mushroom soup
1 package of cheese roll spread (Kraft)
2 Tbls. butter

— Sauté celery, onion, and mushrooms in butter.

— Cook broccoli according to package and drain very well.

— Combine the rest of the ingredients in a Pyrex bowl that may be placed in an oven.

— Heat for 15-20 minutes at 350⁰.

— Serve with chips or veggie dippers.

(You may top this dip with sliced almonds if desired and garnish with paprika and parsley.)

Hot Cheese-Shrimp Dip

2 10 ounce cans cream of shrimp soup
1½ lbs. Swiss cheese, cubed
1 oz. dry vermouth

— Heat undiluted shrimp soup.

— Combine soup, cheese, and vermouth in the top of a double boiler.

— Heat slowly until all of the cheese is melted and all is blended.

— Serve hot with corn chips.

(You might add a can of tiny shrimp, drained, to add chunks of flavor!)

Hot Crab Dip

1 can crab meat, well drained
1 8 oz. package cream cheese, softened
2 Tbls. chopped onion
1 Tbl. milk or cream
1 tsp. salt
Dash of pepper
1 Tbls. horseradish
½ cup sliced almonds

— Blend all of the ingredients, except for the almonds, in a baking dish.

— Top with the sliced almonds.

— Bake at 325⁰ for 20 minutes.

— Serve with fancy crackers.

Hummus Dip

2 cups canned chick peas
1½ tsp. salt
3 cloves garlic, minced
½ - ¾ cup vegetable oil
½ cup lemon juice
2 Tbls. chopped parsley

— Drain chick peas and dry.

— Place all ingredients in a food processor or blender and purée for 30 seconds.

— Scrape down sides and purée until mixture is smooth and creamy.

— Taste and correct seasoning.

— Serve with sesame crackers or vegetable dippers.

Most unique!

Incredible Hot King Crab Dip
(An executive appetizer)

1 pound shelled King crab meat cut into
   1 inch bite-size pieces
2 sticks butter
1 cup dry white wine
Paprika

— Melt butter.

— Place crab in chafing dish and add butter.

— Heat.

— Slowly add wine and taste mixture as you
  pour.

— When it tastes great, stop!

— Sprinkle with paprika.

— Serve in a chafing dish.

Serve warm surrounded by crackers.

People go nuts over this!

Jalapeno Dip

3 Tbls. butter
1 cup chopped onion
1½ cups tomatoes, chopped
4 chopped jalapeno peppers
1 lb. grated sharp Cheddar cheese
Salt and pepper

— Brown onion in butter. Add tomatoes, salt and pepper to taste.

— Simmer until thick.

— Add peppers and cook for 5 minutes.

— Just before serving, heat sauce and stir in cheese until mixture is melted.

— Serve in chafing dish.

Use tostados or large corn chips as dippers.

Liverwurst Dip

½ lb. Liverwurst
1 cup sour cream
1 package dry green onion dip mix
1 Tbl. steak sauce
3 or 4 drops hot pepper sauce

— Combine liverwurst and sour cream, mashing liverwurst with a fork.

— Stir in onion dip mix, steak sauce, and hot pepper sauce.

Serve with rye crackers or on party rye bread.

Mock Guacamole

1 10 ounce package frozen broccoli,
    cooked, drained
½ cup sour cream
2 Tbls. grated Parmesan cheese
2 Tbls. lemon juice
½ small onion

— Place all ingredients in a blender.

— Blend until smooth.

— Serve with corn chips or vegetable dippers.

166

Pickapeppa Dip & Spread

1 8 oz. package cream cheese
¼ cup Pickapeppa sauce

—Pour Pickapeppa sauce on top of cream cheese bar.

—Serve at room temperature.

—Serve on crackers.

Great with cocktails.

Pimiento Cheese Dip

1 jar (2 oz.) pimientos, with liquid, chopped
2 tsps. Worcestershire sauce
½ cup mayonnaise
1 tsp. prepared mustard
1 cup Cheddar cheese, cubed

— Place mayonnaise, pimientos, Worcestershire sauce and mustard in a blender.

— Blend until smooth.

— Add cheese, processing until smooth and creamy.

— Garnish with parsley.

Serve with crackers.

Ranch Veggie Dip

1 package Ranch Style Original Salad
   Dressing
1 cup mayonnaise
1 cup sour cream

— Mix together all ingredients.

— Chill.

— Serve with veggie dippers.

— Garnish with paprika or parsley.

(Good on baked potatoes, too!)

Raw Radish Sauce Dip

1 cup finely chopped radishes
1 8 oz. cream cheese, softened
1 garlic clove, minced
1 Tbl. fresh lemon juice
¾ tsp. salt
½ tsp. dried dillweed
Dash of pepper
(Parsley sprigs and radish slices for garnish)

—Combine chopped radishes, cheese, garlic, lemon juice, salt and dillweed.

—Season with pepper.

—Pour into serving dish and chill for four hours.

—Garnish and serve with crackers or veggie dippers.

So Simple Vegetable Dip

1¼ cups sour cream
1 box dry vegetable soup mix

— Combine sour cream with the soup mix.

— Stir to blend well.

— Refrigerate for a few hours.

Use with veggie dippers.

Spinach & Crab Meat Dip

2 packages frozen chopped spinach
3 green onions and tops
¼ cup Parmesan cheese
1 small can white crab meat
1 stick butter
½ tsp. garlic powder
Tabasco sauce (5 drops)
Salt and pepper to taste

— Melt butter in frying pan.

— Chop onions, add to butter and sauté until soft.

— Cook spinach according to directions - drain well.

— Add to onion mixture, then add all of the other ingredients.

— Serve in chafing dish.

Serve with crackers.

Spinach Dip

1 10 oz. package frozen chopped spinach
  (thawed and squeezed dry)
1½ cups plain yogurt
1 cup mayonnaise
1 package Hidden Valley Ranch Dressing

—Mix all ingredients together.

—Chill.

—Serve with raw vegetables.

Tuna Cream Dip

1 large can tuna, drained & flaked
3 drops hot pepper sauce
1 tsp. grated onion
1 cup dairy sour cream
1 Tbl. drained red caviar

— Combine tuna, pepper sauce, and onion.

— Fold in sour cream.

— Refrigerate.

— Before serving, spoon the caviar on top of dip.

— Garnish with parsley.

Serve with veggie dippers.

Viva La Bean Dip

2 cups cooked black beans
2 cloves garlic, minced
1 pinch saffron
1 tsp. lemon juice
2 Tbls. dry sherry
1 tsp. cayenne

— Drain black beans thoroughly.

— Purée beans in food processor or blender.

— Add garlic, lemon juice, saffron, sherry, and cayenne.

— Mix well. (If it seems dry, add more sherry.)

— Place in bowl and surround with rice crackers and vegetable dippers.

Zucchini Dip

2 small zucchinis
¼ cup unflavored yogurt
2 cloves garlic (minced)
½ tsp. salt

— Finely shred enough zucchini to make 1 cup, firmly packed.

— Place in wire strainer and squeeze out moisture.

— Mix zucchini with other ingredients.

— Chill at least one hour.

— Stir before serving.

— Great with veggie dippers.

— A good fresh summer dip.

SEAFOOD APPETIZERS

Abalone Nibbles

1 can Abalone
¼ cup water
¾ tsp. onion juice
½ cup soy sauce
½ tsp. prepared mustard
Pepper to taste

—Cut abalone in ½ inch squares.

—Combine remaining ingredients.

—Using picks, dip abalone pieces into sauce.

Anchovy Canapes

4 large anchovies
1 8 oz. package cream cheese
4 Tbls. pimiento, chopped
16 toast rounds
3 hard-boiled egg yolks, sieved

— Mash anchovies.

— Blend with cream cheese and pimiento.

— Spread on toast rounds.

— Garnish with egg yolk.

Charlie's Cherry Tuna

2 dozen cherry tomatoes
1 can (4½ oz.) tuna
1 tsp. tarragon
1 Tbl. parsley
¼ cup finely chopped celery
1 tsp. lemon juice
3 Tbls. mayonnaise
2 hard cooked eggs (chopped)

— Carefully slice off top of tomatoes and gently squeeze out juice and seeds.

— Sprinkle lightly with salt.

— Drain tuna and flake.

— Add the tarragon, parsley, celery, lemon juice, mayonnaise, and chopped eggs.

— Stuff the tomatoes with the tuna mixture, forming a dome on top of the tomatoes.

Cheesy Oyster Spread

1 3 oz. package cream cheese
1 4 oz. small jar smoked oysters, drained and
   chopped.
1 Tbl. mayonnaise
1 Tbl. sherry (or milk)
1 tsp. onion juice
½ tsp. paprika
Chives, finely chopped

— Mix together cheese, oysters, mayonnaise,
sherry, onion juice, and paprika.

— Pile into a serving dish.

— Chill.

— Serve with chives sprinkled on top.

Serve with melba rounds or crackers.

Cherry Tomatoes
with Smoked Oysters

36 cherry tomatoes
1 can (3 oz.) tiny smoked oysters, drained

—Wash and stem tomatoes.

—Slice each tomato vertically to within ¼ inch of base.

—Spread apart gently and slip in a smoked oyster.

Cute!

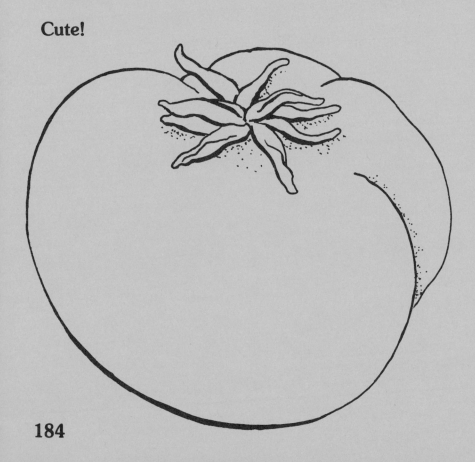

Clam Puffs

1 8 oz. can minced clams, drained
1 3 oz package cream cheese
Dash of Worcestershire
1 tsp. finely grated onion
1 egg white, well beaten
24 crisp crackers

— Combine clams and cheese.

— Add Worcestershire.

— Add onion.

— Fold in egg white.

— Drop by teaspoon onto crackers.

— Arrange on baking sheet.

— Broil until puffy and golden brown.

Crab and Ham
Stuffed Dills

3 - 4 dozen small dill pickles
1 can (4½ oz.) deviled ham
2 Tbls. finely chopped onion
1 can (6½ oz.) crab meat
4 Tbls. mayonnaise
¼ tsp. dill weed
¼ tsp. cayenne
1 tsp. lemon juice

— Slice small dill pickles lengthwise in half.

— Hollow out seeds, etc. to make small boats.

— Blend onion with deviled ham and stuff one half of the pickles.

— Drain crabmeat and add remaining ingredients.

— Fill remaining pickle boats with crab mixture.

— Alternate pickle boats on serving platter.

Crabbie Chestnut Spread

1 lb. crabmeat, chopped or shredded
½ cup minced water chestnuts
2 Tbls. soy sauce
½ cup mayonnaise
2 Tbls. minced green onions

—Combine crabmeat with water chestnuts, soy sauce, mayonnaise and onions.

—Cover and chill overnight.

—Serve with triscuits or crackers.

Crab Stuffed Mushrooms

24 large mushroom caps
Juice of 1 lemon
½ lb. crabmeat
½ cup mayonnaise
¼ cup minced celery
Dash of tabasco
½ cup minced parsley

— Toss mushroom caps in lemon juice.

— Set aside.

— Mix together crabmeat, mayonnaise, celery and tabasco.

— Fill each cap with crab mixture.

— Chill and serve.

— Sprinkle with parsley just before serving.

Crunchy Salmon Spread

16 rounds of bread or toast, buttered
1 1 lb. can salmon, drained and flaked
1 8 oz. can water chestnuts, drained
   and chopped
1 small onion, minced
1 stalk celery, minced
½ cup mayonnaise
2 Tbls. soy sauce
1 Tbl. lemon juice
Parsley, snipped

— Combine all ingredients, except bread.

— Spread salmon mixture on bread or toast
  rounds.

— Sprinkle snipped parsley on top.

Escargot a la Mushroom

24 large mushroom caps
(uniform in size)
1 can of snails - large, cut in half
or small ones, whole
½ cup butter, melted
2 shallots, minced
1 clove garlic, minced
1½ tsp. parsley

— Wash and remove stems of mushrooms.

— Combine butter, garlic, parsley, and shallots.

— Place snail in each mushroom cap.

— Add enough butter mixture to almost overflow.

— Place in deep pans and bake at 350⁰ for 10 minutes until mushrooms are semi-tender and butter is bubbly.

— Serve hot.

Frog's Legs

12 pair of little frog's legs
2 Tbls. lemon juice
Flour
¼ cup butter
2 Tbls. olive oil
1 clove garlic, crushed
2 Tbls. chopped chives
2 Tbls. dry white wine
Salt and pepper

— Sprinkle frog's legs with water and the lemon juice.

— Dry and dust with flour.

— Melt butter.

— Add oil and garlic.

— Sauté for one minute.

— Add chives and frog's legs.

— Shake pan while cooking to help from sticking.

— Turn once.

— When all of this gets to be golden brown, add wine, salt, and pepper.

— You may substitute shrimp or chicken for the frog's legs!

191

Ginger-Garlic Shrimp

2 chopped shallots
2 tsps. minced ginger root
2 cloves minced garlic
2 Tbls. soy sauce
2 tsps. sherry
2 tsps. cooking oil
3 dozen fresh medium shelled shrimp

— Combine all ingredients and pour over the shrimp.

— Marinate ½ hour.

— Shake excess off shrimp.

— Place on rack and broil 2 - 3 minutes on each side.

— Serve hot with toothpicks.

Hot Shrimp Rarebit

1 10 oz. can tomato soup
1 cup grated Muenster cheese
½ lb. minced cooked shrimp
1 Tbl. Worcestershire sauce

— Melt soup and cheese together over low heat.

— Add shrimp and Worcestershire sauce.

— Serve hot with chunks of French bread.

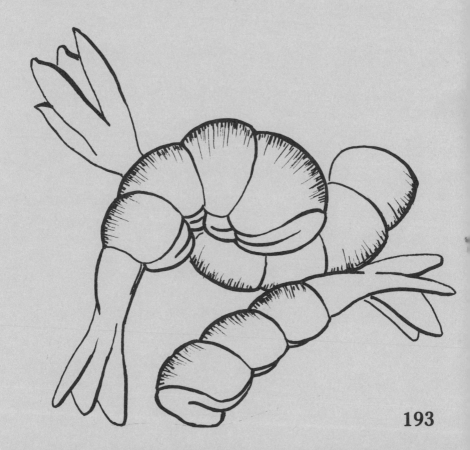

Lobster Bits

8 frozen South African lobster tails
   (4 oz. each)
1 cup Rhine wine
½ cup salad oil
1 Tbl. minced onion
1 tsp. rosemary
¼ tsp. salt
2 tsps. sugar
Dash of black pepper
½ cup melted butter
2 Tbls. lemon juice

—Cook lobster tails as directed, cool.

—Shell and cut crosswise into 1 inch pieces.

—Combine wine, oil, onion, rosemary, sugar, salt, and pepper.

—Pour over lobster bits.

—Chill several hours, turning occasionally.

—Drain and reserve liquid.

—Place lobster in a chafing dish.

—Add ½ cup marinade, butter, and lemon juice.

—Heat and serve with cocktail picks.

Oysters on Horseback

24 large fresh oysters, shelled.
12 strips thin-sliced bacon, cut in half
2 Tbls. lemon juice
2 Tbls. finely chopped parsley
1 tsp. paprika

— Oven at 350°.

— Wrap each oyster with one strip of bacon.

— Secure with toothpick and sprinkle with lemon juice.

— Dust lightly with parsley.

— Sprinkle with paprika.

— Arrange on baking sheet.

— Bake 8 - 10 minutes until bacon is medium crisp.

— Serve warm.

Quick Cold Crab Canape

1 7½ oz. can crab meat
4 sweet pickles, minced
Juice of 1 lime
¼ cup mayonnaise

— Mix crab, pickles, and lime juice.

— Add mayonnaise to moisten.

— Place in bowl surrounded by crackers or spread on crackers and garnish with olive slice or paprika.

Quick Shrimp Sticks

4 slices whole wheat bread
½ lb. shrimp, cooked and peeled
½ small onion
Pinch of ginger
1 tsp. sugar
Dash of salt and white pepper
2 egg whites
Bread crumbs

— Cut each bread slice into 4 strips.

— Combine shrimp, onion, and ginger in blender.

— Chop.

— In bowl, mix egg whites until stiff.

— Add shrimp and spices.

— Spread on bread strips.

— Top with bread crumbs.

— Fry in deep fat till golden brown.

Salmon Cream

½ lb. smoked salmon
1 package (8 oz.) cream cheese
½ cup milk
2 Tbls. chopped chives
2 Tbls. chopped pimiento
¼ tsp. dillweed
1 Tbl. lemon juice
1 dash hot sauce
1 tsp. Worcestershire sauce
2 Tbls. capers
½ tsp. freshly ground pepper

— Combine all ingredients except for capers and pepper in a food processor.

— Purée.

— Scoop into bowl.

— Garnish with capers and pepper.

Serve with pumpernickel pieces.

Salmon Dill Mousse

1 (15½ oz.) can red salmon
3 envelopes unflavored gelatin
¼ cup lemon juice
½ cup peeled, seeded, and chopped
    cucumbers
½ cup chopped onion
½ cup chopped celery
½ tsp. dried whole dillweed
½ tsp. salt
1 cup mayonnaise
1 cup whipping cream

— Drain salmon, reserving liquid.
— Add enough water to the liquid to equal 1 cup.
— Combine liquid with gelatin in a small saucepan.
— Cook over medium heat until gelatin is dissolved.
— Remove from heat - set aside.
— Remove skin and bones from salmon with a fork.
— Place lemon juice, cucumber, onion, celery, salmon, dillweed and salt in a food processor.
— Process till pureed.
— Add mayonnaise and process till well blended.
— Pour in bowl and add gelatin liquid and whipping cream.
— Blend well.
— Pour into 6 cup lightly greased ring mold.
— Chill till firm, unmold and serve with crackers.

Salmon Log

1 can (1 lb.) good pink salmon
2 packages (8 oz.) cream cheese
1 Tbl. minced onion
1 tsp. salt
½ tsp. horseradish
1 tsp. Worcestershire sauce
¼ tsp. liquid smoke
1 Tbl. lemon juice
1 cup chopped pecans
2 tsps. dried parsley
Paprika

— Drain salmon, removing skin and bones.

— Crumble into a bowl.

— Add softened cream cheese.

— Add the remaining ingredients except for pecans and parsley.

— Refrigerate long enough to handle salmon easily.

— Roll into log.

— Roll into pecan and parsley.

— Sprinkle with paprika.

— Serve with crackers.

Salmon Strips

1 tsp. prepared mustard
1 Tbl. butter, softened
4 toasted bread slices, each cut into 4 strips
1 7¾ oz. canned smoked salmon
Stuff green olives, sliced

—Blend mustard with softened butter.

—Spread on toast strips.

—Cover buttered strips with smoked salmon.

—Garnish with stuffed olive slices.

Sardine Spread

1 3¾ oz. can of sardines
1 3 oz. package cream cheese
1½ tsp. grated onion
¼ tsp. garlic salt
Dash of Worcestershire sauce

—Drain sardines and mash.

—Combine sardines with cheese, onion, salt, and Worcestershire sauce.

—Serve on garlic rounds.

Spicy!

Seafood Red Sauce Supreme

1 bottle Delmonte or Heinz Chili sauce
½ cup catsup
2 tsps. horseradish
Juice of one lemon
2 tsps. Worcestershire sauce
4 drops tabasco
1 tsp. salt
Dash cayenne

— Mix all ingredients together.

— Chill.

— Goes well with shrimp or crabmeat.

Seafood Salad Spread

1 cup chopped cooked lobster, crab,
    or shrimp
1 tsp. minced onion
1 cup diced celery
1 tsp. lemon juice
Mayonnaise to bind mixture
Salt and paprika to taste

— Combine all ingredients lightly.

— Chill.

Serve on toasted rounds or crackers.

Shrimp in the Shell

2½ lbs. fresh unpeeled shrimp
4 cans beer
2 cloves garlic
1 bay leaf
2 Tbls. celery seed
1 Tbl. salt
2 Tbls. lemon juice
6 peppercorns
1 Tbl. fresh chopped parsley

— Place all ingredients in a large pot, except for shrimp.

— Bring to boil.

— Add shrimp.

— Boil 4 - 5 minutes until shrimp is a beautiful pink.

— Taste for doneness.

— Drain shrimp.

— Place in bowl filled with crushed ice.

— Serve with Red Sauce Supreme.

Shrimp Paté

3 cups cooked shrimp, minced
2 Tbls. lemon juice
2 Tbls. horseradish
¼ cup chili sauce
½ cup mayonnaise

— Combine all ingredients.

— Chill and serve with cucumber or zucchini slices or crackers.

Smoked Trout Spread

1½ cup flaked smoked trout
1 cup sour cream
1 envelope green onion dip mix
1 tsp. Worcestershire sauce

— Combine trout with sour cream, dip mix, and
  Worcestershire sauce.

— Chill to blend flavors.

— Serve with assorted crackers.

Speedy Shrimp Dip
(No one will believe how good this is!)

One package green onion dip mix
1 cup sour cream
2 8 oz. packages quick frozen small shrimp

— Make dip according to directions by adding sour cream.

— Thaw shrimp and drain very well.

— Add shrimp to green onion dip mix.

— Chill to combine flavors.

— Garnish dip with parsley and paprika.

— Serve with chips.

Sturgeon Surprise

1 loaf pumpernickle party bread
1 small jar caviar
12 thin slices sturgeon (smoked)
1 cucumber peeled and sliced
2 hard cooked eggs
Chives
Butter

— Place small thin slices of smoked sturgeon on small pieces of thinly sliced buttered pumpernickle bread.

— Top with caviar, another slice of sturgeon and paper thin slices of peeled cucumber.

— Sprinkle with chopped hard-cooked eggs (yolk and white chopped separately) and chopped chives.

Tuna Balls

2 13 oz. cans tuna
2 3 oz. packages cream cheese, softened
1 Tbl. lemon juice
2 Tbls. horseradish
¼ tsp. Tabasco sauce
1 cup snipped parsley

— Drain and flake tuna.

— Cream the cheese.

— Add lemon juice, horseradish, tabasco sauce, and tuna.

— Shape tuna cheese mixture into small balls.

— Roll in parsley.

— Chill several hours.

Tuna Dill Spread

1 8 oz. package cream cheese
1 13 oz. can tuna
1 Tbl. dry sherry
1 Tbl. lemon juice
½ tsp. garlic powder
½ tsp. dill weed
⅛ tsp. white pepper

— Rinse and drain tuna.

— Combine all ingredients.

— Beat until light and fluffy.

— Serve on toast or crackers.

Tuna-Fish Cucumber Sandwiches

1 small can tuna fish, drained
1 3 oz. package cream cheese with chives
1 tsp. Season-All
½ tsp. garlic salt
1 package Party-Rye bread
1 cucumber peeled and sliced 1/8" thick
A few stuffed green olives, sliced.
Paprika

—Mix cream cheese, tuna fish and seasonings.

—Spread on each slice of bread.

—Top each slice with cucumber.

—Place olive slice on top of cucumber.

—Sprinkle with paprika.

—Refrigerate.

—Arrange on tray for serving.

Tuna Mushroom Canapés

1 6½ oz. can of tuna, drained and flaked
½ cup mushroom soup
1 Tbl. finely chopped pimiento
1 Tbl. finely chopped green pepper
½ tsp. salt
Paprika to taste
½ cup grated Monterey Jack cheese
12 halved pumpernickel bread slices

—Place tuna in medium bowl.

—Add soup, pimiento, green pepper, salt and paprika.

—Spread on bread.

—Sprinkle with cheese.

—Place on baking sheet.

—Broil three inches from heat for 5 minutes until cheese is golden brown.

Tuna Paté

1 large can tuna, undrained
¼ cup grated onion
1 cup unsalted butter, softened
1/8 tsp. cayenne
½ tsp. dry mustard
¼ tsp. ground cloves

— Place tuna and its liquid with the remaining ingredients in a blender or food processor.

— Cover and process until very smooth.

— Pack into a 2 cup serving bowl and refrigerate overnight.

— Unmold and serve with vegetables and crackers.

— Garnish with softened cream cheese and parsley.

FRUIT AND FRILLS

Fruit Dippers

Cantaloupe
Honeydew
Casaba melon
Pineapple spears
Watermelon balls
Apple wedges
Pear wedges
Strawberries
Grapes
Orange slices
Grapefruit slices
Kiwi fruit
Cherries
Peaches
Nectarines
Apricots
Blueberries
Coconut wedges
Banana slices or spears
Mandarin orange slices
Papaya slices or chunks
Mango slices

Banana Hors d'oeuvres

2 large bananas
1 cup lemon juice
3 oz. cream cheese
⅓ cup chopped nut meats

— Peel bananas and cut crosswise into 1-inch pieces.

— Marinate in lemon juice for 1 hour.

— Drain, cover with cream cheese and roll into nut meats.

— Serve with toothpicks.

Banana Nuts

3 large bananas
½ cup chopped walnuts
1 cup flaked coconut
Juice of 1 lemon

— Peel and slice bananas into 1-inch rounds.

— Set in dish and coat with lemon juice so the banana won't turn brown.

— Roll the banana in the coconut flakes and walnuts.

— Chill.

— Serve with frilly toothpicks.

Banana Scallops

1 egg
1½ tsps. salt
6 firm bananas
¾ cup fine cereal crumbs, bread or cracker
    crumbs

— Beat egg slightly and add salt.

— Slice peeled bananas crosswise into 1-inch
   thick pieces.

— Dip into egg and roll into crumbs.

— Fry in hot oil (375⁰) 1½ - 2 minutes or until
   brown and tender.

— Drain and serve immediately.

Devils on Horseback

24 prunes
12 pieces of bacon cut in half

— Wrap prunes in bacon.

— Secure with toothpicks.

— Bake in **450⁰** oven till bacon is crisp.

— Serve warm.

Fresh Fruit Dipper

⅓ cup sugar
4 tsps. cornstarch
¼ tsp. salt
1 cup unsweetened pineapple juice
¼ cup orange juice
2 eggs, beaten
2 3 oz. packages cream cheese

— Combine dry ingredients in a saucepan.

— Blend in fruit juices.

— Cook, stirring constantly, until thick and bubbly. (5 - 8 minutes)

— Slowly stir some of this hot mixture into the eggs.

— Add egg mixture back into the saucepan and cook over low heat, stirring constantly or until mixture thickens slightly.

— Cool 5 minutes.

— Soften cream cheese and beat into cooled mixture.

— Chill.

Serve with fruit dippers.

Kir Fruit

1 papaya, peeled
2 cups strawberries
2 kiwi fruit
1 cup dry wine
⅓ cup Creme de Cassis

—Cut papaya in half and remove seeds.

—Cut papaya into ¾ inch pieces, set aside.

—Wash strawberries and remove caps.

—Cut in half and add to papaya.

—Peel and thinly slice kiwi.

—Add to papaya mixture.

—Mix wine with Cassis.

—Pour over fruit.

—Cover and refrigerate at least one hour.

—Put in a pretty bowl.

—Serve with toothpicks.

Yellow, green, and red - very pretty!

Melon Balls in Sweet Wine

1 ripe cantaloupe, seeded and made into balls
1 ripe honeydew melon, seeded and made into
　　balls
1 Casaba melon, seeded and made into balls
2 cups sweet white wine
　　(Barsac, Sauternes, or Anjou)
1 tsp. minced candied ginger

— Place the melon balls in a large bowl and add
　the wine and ginger.

— Toss well.

— Cover, refrigerate overnight.

— Serve with frilly toothpicks.

Viva la Vino!

Pecan and Cheese Hors d'oeuvres

16 pecan or walnut halves
½ cup pineapple cheese spread

— Make cheese balls of the spread.

— Press a pecan half on 2 sides.

— Chill.

Pineapple-Macadamia Aloha

1 (1¼ oz. pkg.) blue cheese, crumbled
1 8 oz. pkg. cream cheese
1 Tbls. finely chopped crystallized ginger
¼ cup finely chopped Macadamia nuts
1 (8 oz.) can crushed pineapple, drained

— In a bowl, combine the two cheeses until smooth.

— Stir in ginger, nuts and pineapple.

— Serve with wheat crackers.

Poppy-seed Dressing for Fresh Fruit

1½ cups sugar
⅔ cup white vinegar
2 cups white salad oil
3 Tbls. onion juice
2 tsps. salt
2 tsps. dry mustard
3 Tbls. poppyseeds
4 drops red food coloring

—In a bowl of your electric mixer combine sugar, vinegar and salad oil.

—Mix well until sugar does not seem so granular.

—Add salt, dry mustard, and onion juice.

—Mix well.

—Hand stir in the poppyseeds and food coloring.

—Mix well.

—Refrigerate.

Use as a dip for melon balls or any kind of fruit.

Spiced Pineapple Pickups

1 No. 2½ can pineapple chunks
¾ cup vinegar
1¼ cups sugar
¼ tsp. salt
6 - 8 whole cloves
¼ stick cinnamon
Red or green food coloring

— 2 days ahead, drain syrup from pineapple.

— To ¾ cup syrup add all ingredients except for the pineapple.

— Heat 10 minutes.

— Add pineapple and bring to a good boil.

— Refrigerate.

— Serve with toothpicks or as a garnish.

Strawberries and Cream

1 cup sour cream
1 cup powdered sugar
4 drops red food coloring
1 quart fresh strawberries, washed and hulled

— Mix sour cream, sugar, and food coloring together.

— Chill.

— Serve alongside of the strawberries, using toothpicks to dip.

(This simple dip is good with other types of fruit also).

Tropical Fruit Fluff

1 cup sour cream
¼ cup flaked coconut
2 Tbls. chopped walnuts
2 Tbls. apricot preserves

— Mix all ingredients together.

— If needed, add a few drips of milk to make mixture dipping consistency.

— Chill.

— Serve with chilled fruit as dippers.

Watermelon Basket

1 medium ripe round green watermelon
2 cantaloupes
2 honeydew melons
1 Casaba melon
1 quart strawberries
1 bunch Thompson seedless grapes, green
3 peaches, peeled, sliced and bathed in
    Fruit Fresh

— Cut melon in two pieces, leaving one half deeper than the other.

— Using a melon baller, make watermelon balls, and place in a large bowl.

— Scoop remaining meat out of the bigger half.

— Scallop around top edges of melon to make it pretty.

— Turn it upside down and drain and dry melon bowl.

— Make balls out of other melons.

— Take tops off strawberries, wash and dry.

— Pull grapes off one by one, wash and dry.

— Combine all of the fruit in the big watermelon bowl.

— Serve with toothpicks and have poppyseed dressing nearby.

232

CHICKEN PICKINS PLUS

BBQ Chicken Wings

12 wings with wing tip removed
½ cup honey or
    ¼ cup honey and ¼ cup molasses
2 Tbls. Worcestershire sauce
⅓ cup soy sauce
Juice of one lemon
¼ tsp. ginger
1 clove garlic, minced

—Oven 325°.

—Place wings in a shallow baking dish.

—Mix remaining ingredients and pour over wings.

—Bake one hour.

—Let wings sit in sauce until time to serve.

A little messy, but so good!

Chicken Balls

1 cup pecans, finely ground
1 cup chicken, cooked, finely ground
2 Tbls. pimiento finely chopped
1 Tbl. onion, chopped
¼ tsp. salt
1/8 tsp. hot pepper sauce
½ cup cream of mushroom soup

— Combine ¼ cup of the pecans with the chicken, pimiento, onion, slat, pepper sauce and soup.

— Mix well.

— Make small balls out of the mixture.

— Roll in remaining nuts.

— Cover and chill overnight.

Chicken Bites

3 chicken breasts
2 eggs
Salt
2 Tbls. milk
Red pepper
Self-rising flour
Oil for frying

— Debone and cut 3 chicken breasts into bite-size pieces.

— Sprinkle with salt and red pepper.

— Beat 2 eggs and add the milk.

— Thoroughly coat the chicken in the eggs and milk mixture.

— Dredge in self-rising flour.

— Fry in deep fat until chicken is golden brown.

— Serve with toothpicks.

Chicken Cherries

2 cups shredded cold white chicken meat
1 cup diced celery
1 Tbl. lemon juice
½ cup mayonnaise
3 hard boiled eggs, chopped
1 Tbl. yellow mustard
48 firm cherry tomatoes

— Combine chicken, celery, lemon juice, mayonnaise, eggs and mustard. (You might need more mayonnaise to hold mixture together.)

— Wash and slice in half each cherry tomato.

— Take seeds and mushy part out, leaving pretty red shell.

— Stuff with chicken mixture.

— Garnish with little green olive or paprika.

Chicken-Cucumber Spread

1 cup canned chicken, chopped fine
½ cup finely chopped cucumber
Mayonnaise for blending
½ tsp. Tabasco
½ tsp. Creole seasoning or salt and pepper to
   taste

— Combine chopped chicken and cucumber.

— Blend with enough mayonnaise to hold together.

— Add seasonings.

— Mix well, chill, and serve on crackers.

Chicken Paste

2 Tbls. butter
½ cup chopped blanched almonds
1 whole chicken breast (cooked)
1 Tbl. chopped parsley
1/8 tsp. pepper
2 Tbls. vegetable oil
3 Tbls. dry white wine
2 Tbls. whipping cream

— In small skillet, melt butter.

— Add almonds - sauté until golden brown.

— Set aside to cool.

— Remove and discard bones and skin from chicken breast; chop meat.

— In blender or food procesor combine chopped chicken, sautéed almonds, parsley, salt, pepper, oil, wine, and cream.

— Process until it is almost smooth.

— Serve on toast rounds and garnish.

Chicken Spread

2 cups finely chopped chicken or turkey
    (dark meat)
½ cup chopped ripe olives
Salt and pepper to taste
Mayonnaise to bind

— Combine all ingredients, mixing well.

— Spread on choice of breads or toast.

Chicken Souffles

2 cups minced chicken
1 3 oz. package cream cheese softened
½ cup mayonnaise
1 Tbl. lemon juice
1 Tbl. capers
Dash of Tabasco
Toast rounds

—Mix chicken, cheese, mayonnaise, lemon juice and capers together.

—Add Tabasco.

—Mound onto toast rounds and broil until puffy.

Chicken Wingers

32 chicken wings
⅔ cup melted butter
1 tsp. salt
½ tsp. garlic powder
1½ cups bread crumbs
½ cup grated Parmesan cheese

— Discard wing tips; cut remaining wing into 2 pieces.

— Season melted butter with salt and garlic butter.

— Combine bread crumbs and grated cheese, stirring to mix well.

— Dip wing in butter, then in crumb-cheese mixture.

— Place on a long baking sheet.

— Bake in a 400° oven for 30 minutes.

Chicken and Nut Spread

2 cups white meat chicken, minced
½ can mushrooms, minced
½ cup walnuts, chopped fine
Salt and pepper to taste
Melted butter
Paprika

— Combine minced chicken, mushrooms, and walnuts.

— Season with salt and pepper.

— Moisten with melted butter.

— Sprinkle paprika over mixture.

— Spread on party rye or crackers.

Ginger-Chicken Sandwich Spread

2 3 oz. packages cream cheese
2 4¾ oz. cans chicken spread
4 tsps. finely chopped candied ginger
¼ cup slivered almonds

— Combine all ingredients, blending well.

— Chill at least one hour.

— Spread on toast rounds, crackers or party bread slices.

Very different!

Rumaki

Chicken livers
La Choy water chestnuts
Thin strips of bacon

— Place each water chestnut in a chicken liver.

— Wrap this up in a bacon strip and secure with a toothpick.

— Fry in deep fat until the bacon is crisp.

— Serve hot with a mustard sauce or a sweet and sour sauce.

Smoked Chicken Balls
(or turkey)

1 cup cooked ground chicken or turkey
1 3 oz. package cream cheese
1 Tbl. sour cream
½ tsp. hickory-smoked salt
¼ cup grated Parmesan cheese

— Blend chicken (or turkey), cream cheese, sour cream, and salt.

— Shape into balls 1 inch in diameter.

— Roll each ball in the Parmesan cheese.

— Chill well.

— Serve with toothpicks.

INDEX

CHICKEN PICKINS PLUS

FRUIT & FRILLS

ORDER FORM

You may order as many copies of NIBBLES as you wish for the regular price plus postage and packing. Mail to:

> NIBBLES
> 318 Ila
> Fayetteville, Arkansas 72701

Please mail _____ copies of NIBBLES @ $9.95 each, plus $1.50 postage and packing per book ordered.

Mail books to:

Name _____

Address _____

City, State, Zip _____

ORDER FORM

You may order as many copies of NIBBLES as you wish for the regular price plus postage and packing. Mail to:

> NIBBLES
> 318 Ila
> Fayetteville, Arkansas 72701

Please mail _____ copies of NIBBLES @ $9.95 each, plus $1.50 postage and packing per book ordered.

Mail books to:

Name _____

Address _____

City, State, Zip _____